SHARING IN THE LIFE OF GOD

A Journey into the Real Meaning of Easter

SEAN LOONE

SEAN LOONE

'I am the resurrection and the life. Whoever believes in me even though he dies, yet will he live, and everyone who lives and believes in me will never die'

(John 11: 25-26)

Jesus Christ

SHARING IN THE LIFE OF GOD

This book is dedicated to the NHS and all care workers, especially those who lost their lives in the service of others, during the Coronavirus pandemic of 2020. In you I saw the love of Christ made visible.

'The light shines in the darkness, and the darkness has not been able to overcome it.' (John 1:5)

'This is my commandment: love one another as I have loved you. No one can have greater love than to lay down his life for his friends.'

(John 15:13)

CONTENTS

PREFACE

The Father O'Mahony Memorial Trust

This is a book about Easter and I am writing this preface last of all. One area I have chosen to explore, in detail, is how God, through the resurrection of his son, shares his very life with us. As a result, Easter is something to be experienced. You can imagine my surprise therefore when I came across some of the words of Father Paddy O'Mahony, parish priest of Our Lady of the Wayside from 1962 until his death on Saint Stephen's day in 1991. Introducing the statue of the Risen Christ, by Elizabeth Frink, to the parish he said, **'Every time a prisoner of conscience is liberated, Christ rises again. Every time a woman is able to feed her children, say in Ethiopia, Christ rises again.'** Here then, in these very words you find the essence of what I am trying to say in this book, that the resurrection of Christ is something that we can experience in the here and now.

Father O'Mahony would often talk of the four basic freedoms, which in his opinion, every human being is entitled to and they are,

- **Freedom from Hunger**
- **Freedom from Illness**
- **Freedom from Ignorance**
- **Freedom from Oppression**

i

For him the church, as the body of Christ on earth, does not exist purely for its own sake but rather to recognise and respond to suffering humanity. As a result he would often refer to the balance that needed to be struck between, **'commitment to the family of the parish and the family of humanity,'** which he called **'an enjoyable tension.'** Indeed, the design of the parish church itself bears witness to this with its abundance of plants reflecting the need for the people of God to constantly grow in their understanding and practice of the faith, running water indicating the life-giving power of baptism and views to the outside world showing that the Church is open to all. What this meant was that Father O'Mahony was a priest with a dedicated commitment to justice for the poor, weak and marginalised. Something of which, I have no doubt, the current Pope, Francis, would entirely approve of.

As a result Father O'Mahony set up a **'Justice and Peace'** group, which still operates in the parish today. He also set up a system for collecting surplus medicines from local doctors and pharmacists that would be sorted and catalogued, by volunteers from the parish, before being sent to those people in parts of the world with the greatest need. Collection boxes, for Calcutta, were put at the doors of the Church to remind people, as they entered and left, that to serve the poor and needy is, in fact, to serve Christ himself. These same boxes, with the same message of faith and commitment to the poor, are still there today. There are too many projects Father O'Mahony committed the parish to for me to mention here but from the bushmen of the Kalahari threatened with extinction, to the people of the Turkhana desert in Kenya where a fatal disease threatened to wipe them out if it was not for the parish sending 6,000 vials of the life-saving drug Pentostan, to Sister Sylvia working with the indigenousness Indians of Bolivia, Doctor Towey working in a mission in Uganda alongside Miss Jean Johnson who set up a school there, The Comboni Sisters running a refugee centre in South Sudan and finally the Millhill Fathers working with the oppressed Christians in Pakistan. I think it is safe to say that Father O'Mahony saw it as the duty and obligation of Christians to respond to the needs of suffering humanity. If you ever get the chance to visit the parish Church of Our Lady of the Wayside take the time to look at the arms of the figure of the Resurrected Christ, behind the altar, and see that they are held open in a gesture of welcome. This is the vision Father O'Mahony had for the church and for the parish, that its arms would always be open to those in need.

Sadly in 1991 Father O'Mahony died but in 1994 a Trust was set up in the parish to continue his work. In the same way that he identified the lesser-known cries of the poor, weak and marginalised so the Trust exists to respond to suffering humanity and to do whatever it can to help them. This is why I am donating all the profits from the sale of this book to, **'The Father O'Mahony Memorial Trust,'** something, I believe, he would whole-heartedly approve of. There are, literally, too many names to mention for me when describing the work of the Trust and if I have missed anyone out by name I apologise. However, I would like to mention, in particular, Creina Hearn, Hugh Smith and Maureen Jennings for their long association with and commitment to the work of the Trust.

At the very core of this book you will find an understanding of God who invites us to share in his very life. At Easter when Christ bursts out of the empty tomb shattering Satan, sin and death for all time, he beckons us to life but to life in him. Or putting it another way, to a new way of living, a new way of being, a total participation in God's life and in so doing to be transformed by his grace. We know this is happening when we hear the cries of those less fortunate than ourselves, the cry of suffering humanity itself and just like Our Lord and Saviour our response is one of compassion, generosity and love. As I write these final words I cannot help but feel that Father O'Mahony would approve. My hope now is that in some small way they may also help others grow in their knowledge, understanding and love of the God who shares his very life with us.

Deacon Sean

January 2021

If you would like to find out more about the work of the Trust or make a donation please contact:

'The Father O'Mahony Memorial Trust'

Our Lady of the Wayside Church

Stratford Road

Shirley

Solihull

West Midlands

B90 4AY

Ourladyofthewaysidechurchshirley.co.uk

olw.shirley@rcaob.org.uk

INTRODUCTION

This book is about God and his Son, Jesus Christ. I wanted to make that clear from the start so that there is absolutely no confusion. It is also about Easter the biggest life-transforming event in the history of the universe. However, it is not an apology for Christianity, in fact the reverse is true, in so far as, it is a proclamation of Christianity's most central and life-giving truth. That God became a human being, just like us, that he lived a life, just like us, that he died a death, just like us, but that death could not hold him and he rose to new life and in so doing recreated everything. Most people are, perhaps, to some degree aware of this, albeit in a vague sort of way but it seems to have little impact on the way in which they live their lives. So inspired by the grace of the Holy Spirit I wanted to do something about it, hence this book.

My starting point was, in fact, Christmas Eve, when I found myself, fairly late in the day if I am honest, in my local supermarket and what I found there, literally, stopped me dead in my tracks and made me think, 'what is going on?' You see what I observed were the shop assistants taking down all of the Christmas decorations before Christmas had even happened. Then to my horror I saw, through an open door in the stock room, a pallet of Easter eggs! As if that was not enough, I then noticed another shop assistant removing the Christmas cards and replacing them with ones for none other than Saint Valentine's Day. Was this, I thought, what our Christian feasts and festivals have been reduced to? That somehow they have been stolen by the commercial world before being repackaged and sold at a profit to those who have been convinced that this is what they are really about? Then one day, perhaps, Christmas and Easter will become like Stonehenge one of the world's most well-known and greatest ancient monuments. We know it is there and we may even like to visit it from time to time but we have not got a clue as to why it was built and how important it was to our ancient ancestors.

This book then is an attempt to set the record straight about Easter. You will not find anything in it about the Easter bunny, Easter bonnets or Easter eggs but you will find an exploration as to why **EASTER** is **THE** most important festival in the Christian calendar. Equally and at the same you will also discover why Easter is for all people, God leaves no one out. Right from the start emphasis will be placed on how each and every single one of us can experience, in our own lives, the reality of Easter in the here and now and how this can lead to what I call transformed existence or a complete change in the way in which we live. The focus of our exploration and upon whom everything, literally, depends is Jesus Christ and our journey will draw us closer and closer to him. This is why the Bible will be our primary source of information; so if you have one, then keep it close by.

I have referred, in the title of this book, to a journey into the real meaning of Easter and now I want to explain why. My home parish Church is called 'Our Lady of the Wayside' and it was built as part of the Second Vatican Council's Liturgical reforms in 1965. As you enter the church on your right hand side you will see the baptistery with its stone font on a small island surrounded by water, all encased by beautiful stained glass windows. Baptism is the beginning of our Christian journey of faith and although you can be baptised at any age, for most of us, it takes place when we were very young. You are now standing in the narthex of the church with a small day chapel on your left. Walking forward and also on your left hand side, built into the brick wall, is an image of the crucified Jesus with his head falling forward and his hair covering his face. It is a poignant reminder of the pain, suffering and humiliating death he had to go through and, as such, demands our attention. As we move from the narthex into the main body of the Church our focus is then drawn first to the large stone altar, which dominates everything and then behind it, to an image of the resurrected Christ bursting out of the tomb complete with the wounds, on his body, from his crucifixion. Standing in that narthex I remember, one day, having a moment of inspiration. The very design of the church actually reflected our own journey through life and, at the same time, corresponded with not only the life of Christ but also with a journey into the real meaning of Easter. Let me explain. Life for all of us begins with birth, followed for some of us with baptism, where not only our journey through life begins but also our journey into the real meaning of Easter whether we realise it or not, also starts. Standing at that font told me that. Then we live and for all of us there will be no doubt, moments of real pain, misery and suffering. In the end, as we all know, there will be death. Standing in front of the crucified Christ built into that brick wall also told me that. However, as I entered the main body of the Church and saw the image of the resurrected Christ I was also confronted with another truth, that death is, in fact, not the end but only the beginning of a new life. Then something else also struck me that the journey we make through life, we do not make alone because God through his son has made that journey too. Every step we take, he takes with us, every pain we suffer, he suffers too and then, just as we think everything is over and the darkness of death threatens to overwhelm us, we discover that he is risen and that his life, given to us as a free gift, is stronger than the grave. This is the power of the Easter message, it is written into the fabric of my own parish church but it is also written into the fabric of our own lives too. Here we find the reason why I have written this book, which is to reawaken within us our awareness of this truth.

When I shared my desire to write this book with members of the church I very much admired and respected, their response was, shall we say, less than enthusiastic. 'You are wasting your time. No one will buy it, no one will read it and as a result no publisher will touch it!' Hardly words of inspiration. Despite this, however, I believed passionately in two things. Firstly in God, if he inspired me, by the grace of his Holy Spirit, to write this book then that is exactly what I would do. Secondly, I believed in people, God's people, which, in fact, include all people because God excludes no one. You see what I believe is that God's life and our lives are bound together to the point that they cannot be separated. As a result everything we experience in life, God in and through the life and death of his son experienced too. This is why I have stressed how important it is to search for God in the very place, perhaps, where we would least expect to find him, that is, in our own experiences. If we can do that, I promise you something wonderful will happen as we make our journey into the real meaning of Easter because we will discover that we are, doing nothing less, than **'Sharing in the Life of God.'**

I find myself writing these introductory words during the lockdown period of the Coronavirus in May 2020. The news reminds us constantly of the NHS and other care workers who, literally, day after day are putting their own lives on the line simply to care for others. Some of these, sadly, have, through holding out the helping hand of love lost their own lives. Here I am reminded of the words of Jesus when he said,

'No one can have greater love, than to lay down his life for his friends' (John 15:13)

Our lives and the life of God cannot be separated from each other. From our common birth to the pain of the cross, experienced by us in life, to the realisation that with death actually comes life, new life. This is the Easter message and I invite you now, the reader, to join me as we make a journey into its real meaning and to discover that, literally, every day we are, in and through the life, death and resurrection of Jesus Christ, actually, **'Sharing in the Life of God.'**

Deacon Sean Loone

CHAPTER ONE

Touching God

'There are spaces of sorrow only God can touch.'

Lord, touch these places in our hearts.

Sr. Helen Prejean

Recently I had a conversation with a colleague about the people I work most closely with in my ministry. It soon became clear that they all had something in common in that each and every single one of them was, in fact, to a greater or lesser extent broken by life. As the conversation went on something dawned on me and not for the first time that we are all, in some way, damaged by life and therefore we all are in need of healing; otherwise why would we need God? Yet we also need to recognise this and have both the strength and the character to simply ask for help. However, to do this I am going to suggest something, which, I believe, is vitally important if we are ever going to be healed, and that is, we need to learn to look at life from the inside out. Only then can things change. Only then will we ever be able to be transformed and only then will we really be able to discover who we are and so truly find the wholeness that we all seek.

The key to understanding this for me is suffering. My proposal is a simple one, that suffering is the fundamental problem of the human race and that we should focus all of our time, effort and resources on identifying and relieving suffering in all of its many and diverse forms. However, if we are ever going to achieve this the starting point has to be with love and this opens the door for God; for God loves us unconditionally and we see this most clearly in the life, death and resurrection of his Son, Jesus Christ. You see in and through Jesus, who became one of us and one with us God came to love us from the inside out. Indeed God will do what we were incapable of doing, save us from ourselves and in the process do away with both suffering and death. This is something only God could do but he had to become one with his people first. He had to suffer like us and he had to die like us, everything had to be done from the inside out and here lies the key to understanding why God had to become human, suffer and die, whilst at the same opening up the way for revealing that they best way to follow him and therefore to be a human being, is through the compassion, mercy, forgiveness and love of his Son.

This is where everything began to change for me by being confronted with suffering, especially innocent suffering. I have written extensively about suffering in my previous book, **'Only in the Crucified God – Questions and Answers on Faith, Hope and Love,'** but now I want to be able to look at it in a slightly different way by focusing on two things, firstly the need to see everything, including suffering, from the inside out. Unfortunately most of us, I believe, are simply too afraid to do this because we have never been shown or told how. Then secondly to see how this can lead to a new way of living or being, called transformed existence.

So what do we need to do now is the next most important question to ask. If, however, we are to make any progress in understanding what this actually means in the reality of our everyday lives then what I am proposing, in this book, is that the key to understanding everything is, Jesus. In the book of Revelation, the very last book in the Bible Jesus says, **'I am the alpha and the omega, the beginning and the end,'** (21:6) The closer, therefore, we stay to Jesus, the deeper we will be drawn into both the mystery of God and into understanding what it is to be really human and therefore truly alive. For only in Christ is the fullness of human life revealed (Colossians 2:9-10). Therefore we need to keep three things constantly in mind as we journey through the pages of this book,

1. To value our own experiences of life as the unique place where we can encounter the living God.
2. Be prepared to see everything from the inside out the starting point for which is our own life.
3. To work towards an understanding that by God's grace our lives can be transformed.

We then need, as a starting point, to take all of this and simply apply it to suffering.

Our journey begins, then, with Jesus on the bank of the river Jordan. Unlike his cousin John the Baptist Jesus leaves the desert and makes his way into the foothills of Galilee, the very place where he grew up. It is the land of Zebulun and Naphtali, where people, according to the prophet Isaiah, **'walked in darkness.'** (Isaiah 8:23 – 9:3) Jesus knows the people well and how much they are suffering. Two things have been crippling them for so long, firstly debt as Rome, King Herod and the Temple authorities in Jerusalem taxed them and secondly hunger as a direct consequence of financial hardship. These were people who were desperately poor and struggling with life. Disease and infant death was common; housing was of a low standard and therefore life hard. The area was a hotbed for civil unrest as young men took to the hills with the intention of making Rome pay for their occupation of the land, which by right belonged to the people of God. Equally this was the land where many pagans, those who were not Jews had settled and where they had made their home. All of this gave rise to the area having a reputation for itself, especially amongst the religious and aristocratic elite in Jerusalem, who considered the Galilee to be a place full of ignorant peasants who had lost their faith in God. There was, however, worse to come in so far as the poor, crippled and diseased of the day were classified as sinners by their own religious leaders, a group known as the Pharisees with whom Jesus had several clashes. Putting it simply, to be placed into one of these groups meant that you, your parents or your grandparents must have committed some sort of sin, which had offended God. Hence your ailment was an external sign of your punishment from on high, which, in turn, only God and God alone could ever forgive. As a result the Pharisees taught that all these groups of people were rejected, abandoned and unwanted by God and if God treated them like that it was everyone else's religious duty and obligation to do the same.

I said earlier in this chapter that the key to understanding our humanity was suffering so what happens next will be crucial to my line of thought. The first thing to note, however, is what Christians actually believe about Jesus, that he is fully God and fully human in one and the same person. The second thing to take on board is the distance that had grown between humanity and God as a result of the fall of Adam and Eve. Putting it simply they, as representatives of the human race, made a conscious decision to reject God. In many ways the whole of the first half of the Bible is an exploration of the consequences of this act and of God's continued and repeated attempts to call them back to him. For, in truth, and as we have already seen God never stopped, unconditionally, loving his people. In the end, however, the self-inflicted wound of sin was too deep and the distance too great for humanity to be able to elicit any kind of repair by itself, only God could do that but he would have to do so from the inside out. In other words God would have to become one of us and one with us to heal the wounds of sin but he will do so from within his own creation, those made in his own image, namely us. This is exactly what I mean when I say from the inside out. Hence in Jesus, God would share our humanity and heal the wounds of sin but from within and in so doing reveal the true nature and being of God. This brings us back to suffering and how Jesus responds to this will change everything.

The first words uttered by Jesus in the Gospel of Matthew are, **'Repent, for the Kingdom of Heaven is close at hand.'** (Matthew 4:17) What Jesus meant here putting it quite simply, is that if we are to truly recognise God and so be transformed by his grace what is needed is a complete change of heart. Or putting it another way we need to see things from the inside out, which requires us to see life in a completely different way. Having established that Jesus is both God and human in one and the same person and that he has come to save the human race from the inside out by literally suffering and dying with them and that if we are ever going to understand what any of this means we need to stay close to him, then what Jesus does next will be crucial.

The first thing we need to do is to keep our fundamental premise in the forefront of our mind, which is that suffering is the core problem of the human race. We also need to understand that God and therefore Jesus does not will, desire or seek suffering and therefore neither should we. Our next premise is to purport that Jesus, as the Son of God, comes to deal with suffering but does so from the inside out, that is by becoming one of us and one with us. Indeed this will eventually lead, in fact, to his own death. However, for now let us follow him into the foothills of the Galilee and observe what happens. It is interesting to note that Jesus avoids the large towns and cities and instead concentrates his attention, for the most part, on the much smaller villages similar to the one he grew up in, Nazareth. Here he seeks out the lost, the abandoned, the crippled, the diseased, all those who were rejected, despised, unwanted and unloved by the society in which they lived. All those who had been told by their own religious leaders that they were sinners, punished by God for their sins and who, as a result, were simply not wanted. In other words they were suffering and were without hope, living for the most part, therefore, in a state of despair.

Then along comes Jesus, actively seeking out suffering humanity amongst the people he had grown up with and knew well. It is now we get an insight into his reaction to all those who suffer. The prophet Hosea put it like this when describing God's reaction to what he expects from his people, **'For I desire, mercy not sacrifice.'** (Hosea 6:6) Jesus quotes the same passage in Matthew when he says, **'My pleasure is in mercy, not sacrifice.'** (Matthew 9:13) What we are beginning to see here through Jesus is nothing less than the will of God, being revealed from the inside out because what happens next is literally earth shattering. Jesus finds suffering humanity and assures it of two things,

1. That God loves them, unconditionally.
2. That they are not only assured of a place in the Kingdom of Heaven but that they will be first.

This of course brought Jesus into direct conflict with the religious leaders of the day who taught the exact opposite and their approach to the same issue was completely different. The Pharisees saw externally what they believed were signs of sin which, in effect, alienated people from God. Jesus on the other hand looked at suffering humanity with the eyes of God's mercy, compassion, forgiveness and love. Jesus saw through to the heart and revealed God's desire to illuminate all forms of suffering. In essence Jesus was revealing in the midst of humanity or if you will from the inside out, that sin in all its varied forms can never succeed in blocking us from God. Let us now, therefore, have a deeper look at how this worked in practice.

The Healing of the Paralysed Man (Mark 2:1-12)

Jesus goes to Capernaum and is teaching in a house surrounded by a large group of people. Outside four friends are trying to get a paralysed man to Jesus in the hope that he can do something for him. We now know, of course, that such a person would have been classified as a sinner by the religious leaders of the day. Outside, the friends carrying the paralysed man become frustrated, as they cannot get him into the house because of the large crowd. So ingeniously they climb onto the roof, remove the tiles and let the paralysed man down to where Jesus is. What happens next is quite remarkable in relation to what we have said so far because Jesus actually says to the paralysed man, **'My child your sins are forgiven.'** (Mark 2: 5) Immediately there is a response from some of the religious leaders who are present, **'How can this man talk that? It is blasphemy!**

Who can forgive sins but God alone?' Of course to them this makes complete sense, as all they can see are the external signs of paralysis, which must mean sin, which, in turn, reflects punishment from God. If this is true, then surely only God can forgive such sins? So Jesus responds with a challenge, '**Which is easier: to say to the paralytic, "Your sins are forgiven" or to say, "Get up pick up your mat and walk?" But so that you may know that the Son of man has the authority to forgive sins on earth – he said to the paralytic – 'I say to you: get up, pick up your mat, and go off home.'** (Mark 2: 5-11) Here we see Jesus clearly relieving the pain, misery and suffering of the paralysed man and in so doing revealing the compassion, mercy and forgiveness of God. Or in other words what we see here, right before our very eyes, is the nature of God who not only heals and forgives the paralysed man from the inside out but who, at the same time, does so in the midst of humanity. For God does not desire suffering but rather that it be illuminated through acts of mercy, compassion and forgiveness but above all love. There can be little doubt that the paralysed man's life was transformed by his encounter with Jesus. Indeed, the Gospel passage we have just explored ends like this, '**And the man got up, and at once picked up his mat and walked out in front of everyone, so that they were all astonished and praised God saying, 'We have never seen anything like this.'** (Mark 2:12)

Such a reading challenges us to respond and reflect on how we should react to the suffering we are surrounded by today.

Furthermore, to ask how we might see things from the inside out and so co-operate with God to illuminate the pain, misery and suffering in the world around us now. The final challenge is to recognise how our own lives may be transformed by God's grace as a result of meeting and serving him in those around us who know only pain, misery, suffering and rejection.

Touching God (Matthew 25: 31-46)

At the very core of this book can be found three fundamental principles. The first is that it is possible to encounter God in and through our own experiences of life. The second is that we need to learn how to see things from the inside out by not being obsessed with the external world in which we live and the third and final thing is to believe how if we can follow this pattern of living, our lives will be transformed by God's grace.

Some time ago at the end of a talk I was giving on scripture to a group of young people I was asked a most challenging question, 'If you had to identify one thing that made a person a Christian, what would it be?' It made me pause because I wanted to offer at least two parts to my answer but the questioner remained most insistent, 'What one single thing, in your opinion, made a person a Christian?' The answer I gave, in the end, surprised many and shocked some because this was my reply, 'In my opinion that one single thing which made a person a Christian more than anything else was their willingness to put other people before themselves.' The reason why people were so shocked and surprised was because they expected me, in my answer, to go straight for belief in God or Jesus. So when asked, my qualification for my answer was this, that to put other people before ourselves is to reveal the nature and the being of God as revealed by Jesus Christ. This is something that we have already remarked on, in so far as, it was the way in which Jesus revealed the nature of God as being the God of mercy, compassion, forgiveness and love when he healed the paralysed man. In other words when the crowd saw Jesus heal the paralysed man, responding to his pain, misery and suffering, then there, right before their very eyes, they were observing, nothing less, than God healing humanity from the inside out. In and through Jesus and his actions God touches our wounds too and heals them but equally, the crowd, if only they had recognised who he was could also have reached out and touched him and in so doing, touch God himself.

Turning to the Gospel of Matthew we have a marvellous parable told by Jesus called, **'The Sheep and the Goats.'** (Matthew 25: 31-46). At the end of time Jesus divides humanity into two groups, the sheep and the goats. The sheep are people who without any prior knowledge or thought recognise and serve Jesus in the hungry, the thirsty, the stranger, the naked, those who are sick and those who are in prison, or in other words suffering humanity. However, the sheep express surprise that such actions correspond to God's will by asking, **'When did we see you hungry and feed you, or thirsty and give you a drink? When did we see you a stranger and**

welcome you, needing clothes and we clothed you? When did we see you sick or in prison and go to you? (Matthew 25: 37-38) Then remarkably Jesus replies, **'In so far you did this to one of the least of these brothers and sisters of mine, you did it to me.'** (Matthew 25:39) Or in other words to love and to serve people in need is, in effect, to love and to serve God.

To understand the full depth of this and the implications of what it means we need to be clear about exactly the claims we are making. God invites us to participate in nothing less than his life through the love and service we give to each another. Jesus reveals the nature of God by seeking out suffering humanity and responding with acts of compassion, mercy, forgiveness and love. Such love is, in fact, unconditional in so far as it has no strings attached. We are called to love in the same way. God loves like this not because we deserve it but simply because we need it and that brings us back to one of the first points made earlier in this chapter that we all are broken by life and in need of healing. You see what God does in his Son is incarnate, makes flesh and blood, his mercy and love. Later Jesus will send out his disciples with a mission and that is to alleviate human suffering and in so doing bring new life to a broken world. They will proclaim that the Kingdom of God is near, cure the sick, raise the dead, cleanse those suffering with leprosy and cast out evil. God's love has been given to them freely now they are to give freely in return.

Perhaps part of our problem today is that we have forgotten how to love like this but the way back is clear and that is through faith in Jesus. Recognising that the key to understanding everything is suffering we need to learn to look at people like Jesus did and, at the same time, treat people like he did. You see, as we have already said, Jesus looks at people with the eyes of tenderness, mercy and compassion. So to imitate him is, in effect, to become more human, to become what we were always destined to be. This, of course, requires us both to think and act differently but the process begins from within each and every single one of us. There is here a challenge, which is to recognise God in suffering humanity and serve him there, to refuse to do so is, in effect, to turn our backs on the crucified one. In many ways this is a radical call to a revolution whose primary aim is to liberate humanity from suffering. But the revolution is one of love, mercy and compassion for all people.

This is how it works in action. Firstly we have to engage with our own experiences of life, whatever they may be, and have the courage to really open our eyes and recognise suffering in all its forms as the most fundamental problem of the human race. Secondly we have to recognise, appreciate and understand, that this can only be done from the inside out or in other words our hearts have to be touched by the suffering of others to the point that we are moved to do something about it. Such action, in whatever form it takes, which alleviates the pain, misery and suffering of our fellow human beings leads to our own lives being transformed by God's grace because in the words of Jesus, to love and to serve others is to love and to serve

God.

Now we are ready to go back to the question we explored earlier, the one I was asked by a young person after the talk I gave on scripture, **'If you had to identify one thing that made a person a Christian, what would it be?'** Do you remember what my answer was that some of those present found so shocking and others so surprising? Well it was this, **'In my opinion, that one thing which made a person a Christian more than anything else was their willingness to put other people before themselves.'** I hope that by now you, the reader, can understand a little more about why I gave this answer. Yet there is still one more thing I need to explain before I can end this first chapter.

We all, perhaps, know people, from our own lives, who put others before themselves. Once again, in my previous book, **'Only in the Crucified God – Questions and Answers on Faith, Hope and Love,'** I wrote extensively about the key role my own Mother played in this capacity in my life. Equally, I know a man who would not describe himself as religious by any means and yet he dedicates the whole of his spare time to helping the homeless and the destitute. There are in fact countless people who simply through acts of kindness, generosity and what I can only describe as love reach out to and literally serve people in need. Here I cannot help but call to mind the image of Jesus on his knees washing the feet of his disciples and the words of his parable, **'The Sheep and the Goats'**, when he said, **'In so far you did this to one of the least of these**

brothers and sisters of mine, you did it to me.' (Matthew 25:39) When I see actions such as these I cannot help but feel humbled, it is as if in them I am actually witnessing the love of God himself. To this end, it is almost like you can reach out and touch God in the loving actions expressed by such people. What I am saying here is, I hope, something simple but also profound in so far as when people act like this they are literally incarnating, making physically present, nothing less than the love of God. In this away the full potential of our humanity is revealed. This is how it works; firstly a person's heart is touched, on the inside, by experiencing human suffering. This then moves them to acts of compassion, on the outside, revealed by responding to that suffering. The final part of the process is that as a result of what has happened their lives are transformed by God's grace, their humanity has been enhanced and the potential for the human race realised. This, in effect, was exactly what Jesus was saying in the parable of **'The Sheep and the Goats'.** Or putting it another way Jesus was saying, join me in realising the Kingdom of Heaven, in the here and now. Identify all those who are suffering in anyway and do whatever you can to help them. If we could only grasp the fullness of this and what Jesus actually meant when having washed the feet of his disciples he said to them, **'I give you a new commandment: that you love one another; you also must love one another just as I have loved you.'** (John 13:34) I would ask you now, the reader, just to take a moment out and reflect on all those people who you know or have known, who in any way have acted in a selfless way by relieving the suffering, pain and misery of others. The only explanation I can find that satisfies my question as to why people would possibly do this is, love. For me God is, of course, the source of all love and we see this most clearly revealed in his Son, Jesus. Therefore to see such love in action before our very eyes is for me in a real sense, to see the love of God made visible, something we can reach out and in a very real and meaningful sense, touch. Think of charity workers who go willingly to some of the most dangerous places on earth simply to relieve the pain, misery and suffering of some of the most wretched people on the planet. Then think of parents who literally give up everything to look after their disabled son or daughter. The list is endless but the message remains the same that which makes us most human is to relieve the pain, misery and suffering of our fellow human beings. However, I would also add to this that such actions also conform us most closely, as we have seen, to the will of God.

I want to end this chapter though with a concrete example of what we have been exploring. If there is one event, which stands out in modern times that reveals the potential for evil in the human heart, then it has to be the Holocaust. This has to be the example, which confronts humanity with not only suffering but also innocent suffering and, as such, demands a response. Such a response is beyond the scope of this book but it needed to be acknowledged and there is still a great need to accept responsibility for the Holocaust by the human race, if there is ever going to be true healing to the great wound it has left. I will, however, try humbly to shed some light on this dark chapter of our history.

In 1943, in Auschwitz, one of the Nazis most notorious death camps up to 1,000 Jews were being killed every day. One of the prisoners was a Catholic priest called Maximilian Kolbe. The guards would regularly visit the cells and take away men for execution. One such man was called Francizek Gajowniczek, who when chosen begged the guards not to take him because he had a family consisting of his wife and children. At this point Maximilian stepped forward and volunteered to take the place of the man, to which the guards readily agreed. He was then taken away with a group of other men and placed in an underground cell where they were all left to starve to death. For the next two weeks those who passed the cell could hear Maximilian praying and singing with his fellow prisoners. One by one they all died until in the end only he was left. Finally the guards entered the cell and killed him by way of lethal injection. In 1982 Maximilian Kolbe was made a saint by the Catholic Church and on that day in Saint Peter's square, in Rome, Francizek Gajowniczek, the man for whom Maximilian gave up, willingly, his own life, wept.

I include this true story to illustrate my main point that when confronted with suffering, especially innocent suffering, God invites us to respond with acts of compassion, mercy, forgiveness and love. Maximilian Kolbe did exactly this. He brought light, where there was only darkness and love where there was only hate. His actions, of course, did not end the war nor did they close the concentration camps but surely in them we can see how the love of God is revealed? Once again Maximilian's heart must have been touched as he witnessed the suffering of others. What followed was, in effect, a sacrifice, an external act of love, whereby he literally gave up his life so that a fellow prisoner might live. Jesus once said, **'Greater love has no man than this that he lay down his life for his friends.'** (John 15:13) In that evil place others saw the actions of this man, which conformed completely not only with the words of Jesus but with his actions too. In such a place that knew only cruelty, pain, suffering and death the love of God was made visible in Maximilian to the point that it touched the heart of Francizek Gajowniczek and transformed his life forever.

In this chapter we have tried to explore how our response to suffering defines who we are as human beings made in the image of God. The story of Maximilian Kolbe, at the very least, tells us that no matter how dark things become there is always the light of hope. The truth is that through Jesus God invites us to join him in a revelation of his love for all people. To achieve this we must not be immune to the suffering of our fellow human beings nor must we let suffering in all its varied forms disguise itself. Instead we are invited to join Jesus in his mission of healing tenderness, a mission, which includes everyone and excludes no one. When this happens God is made visible and we can literally reach out and touch him with our hearts.

CHAPTER TWO

Good News

'Everyone who listens to these words of mine and acts on them will be like a sensible man who built his house on rock.'

Matthew (7: 24-27)

If we are to make any progress in our journey into the real meaning of Easter then it is essential that we be prepared to invest time, energy and effort in the project. Nowhere is this more important than the Bible, which for the Christian is nothing less than the word of God. For the most part in our journey we will be concentrating our attention on the New Testament with particular emphasis on the Gospels. This, however, is where the problem actually begins because we have lost touch with the vital role God's word should play in our lives. Take for example our brothers and sisters of the Muslim faith. Their holy book is called the Qur'an and is revered as the perfect word of God. When the Qur'an is in a room, with other books, it must be placed on the highest shelf to highlight how far it is above all other written words. Very often the book is covered with a cloth, kept in a special place and treated with the utmost dignity and respect. Moving on to our brothers and sisters of the Jewish faith. One of their holy scriptures is called the Torah and consists of the first five books of the Hebrew Scriptures called by Christians the Bible. It is, in fact, written out by hand, which takes several years to complete. In the synagogue the Torah is kept in a cupboard called the tabernacle, it is highly decorated often with bells attached so that people are aware when it is being moved. At the same time it is not unusual for people to kiss the Torah as it represents the closest thing on earth to God. Finally, again as a mark of respect and to preserve the text, a metal finger called a 'Yad' is used to trace the words as they are read out in the synagogue. Equally a 'Mezuzah' is a small box attached to the door frame of many Jewish homes, on the inside of which is a prayer called the 'Shema' taken from the book of Deuteronomy and expressing the essence of Judaism, simply that God must be loved and obeyed above all other things. The box is touched lightly with the fingers on entering or exiting the home, after which the lips are also touched symbolically representing that the word of God should be in the mouth of the believer at all times. Compare this now with our lack of respect for the Bible. I have found myself in schools, for example, with Bibles scattered all over the floor, with pages torn out and with words of disrespect written all over the text! Here I am not pointing the blame at anyone but just stating the facts as I have experienced them. What is missing though is a serious lack of appreciation, love and respect for God's most sacred and holy word, which has to be down to poor formation. Before you, the reader, proceed with reading the rest of this chapter and indeed book I would suggest that you make sure you have access to the Bible or at least the New Testament. If finance is a problem the 'Gideon's' will provide copies of the Bible or New Testament completely free of charge. Or you can get a paper back copy of a gospel from the Bible Society for about £1. If all of these avenues prove fruitless you can always see if a friend has a copy they can let you have, saving that try your local library or church. Ultimately there can be no substitute for you experiencing God's word directly for yourself; you might even be amazed at what happens.

It is not, however, all doom and gloom. As a deacon within the Roman Catholic Church one of my roles is to carry the book of the gospels, in procession, as we enter the church for mass. I deliberately hold the book in an elevated way so that all those present can see it as being special. It is then placed gently on the altar, which for Catholics is a very important part of the church as it is where Holy Communion is celebrated. The point being made here is that God is as present in his word as he is in the most blessed and holy sacrament of Holy Communion. When I retrieve the book two candle bearers will accompany me and sometimes there will be incense too. I then, with the book of the gospels elevated once more, make my way to the raised lectern from which it will be read. However, before its proclamation I carefully trace the sign of the cross over the text with my thumb before doing the same on my forehead, lips and over my heart. Here I am asking that the word of God be in my mind, issue forth from my mouth and stay close to my heart. At this point the book may also be incensed, which again serves to highlight its importance. Finally having read the text I will reverence the page with a simple kiss. All the way through then God's word is being honoured and respected for all to see, understand and know its significance and importance in the life of God's people today. This practice, however, is something that we must all learn to carry into and replicate in our everyday lives.

Now I think we are ready to move on. If we went back to the early days of Christianity there was a huge respect for God's word, this, in fact, is what Jesus himself had to say, **'Heaven and earth will pass away, but My words will never pass away.'** (Matthew 24:35) The disciples of Jesus and many of those who lived in Galilee had seen for themselves what Jesus could do with words, the sick were healed, sinners were forgiven, fear banished and God's love assured for all. Those same early Christians fed off Jesus's words as their hearts burned within them and their lives transformed forever.

At first the words of Jesus were passed on simply by word of mouth something called the oral tradition but very early on these same words were seen as being so precious that the disciples began to collect them. Every letter, every word and every sentence would have been seen to be vital and life giving so that their preservation would have been identified as being essential to the life of the church. Yet the major difference with Jesus, of course, is that Christians believed he was alive. Thus they were not simply collating the words of a dead man but of the living God. In fact these words of their living Lord and Master were believed by those early Christians to be infused with his very life; '**The word of God is something alive and active.**' (Hebrews 4:12) Equally they found in them instructions as to how God actually wanted them to live, '**This is my commandment: love one another, as I have loved you.**' (John 15:12) The problem for us today, however, is that many of us are too familiar with these words; we have lost a sense of their total and utter uniqueness, in so far as nothing like them had ever been said before. The idea that God could love all people unconditionally and that to reveal the depth of that love he would, literally, become one of them and die the humiliating death of a common criminal on a cross was so, outrageously unheard of, its origins could not have come from humanity but only from God. This is why I would contend that the words, which describe such momentous events that can only be found in the Gospels, give rise to nothing less than a new literary genre. This is how special and unique these words are and this is why they deserve nothing less than the utmost dignity and respect from us. In describing how Jesus became one of us Saint John actually put it like this, '**The word became flesh, he lived among us.**' (John 1:14)

Those early Christians understood this all too well. When they came together and shared the word of God, they believed that they were hearing the words of their living Lord speaking directly to them because he was, in fact, not dead but alive; '**Lord, to whom shall we go? You have the words of eternal life.**' (John 6:68) Think of it like this, when we are listening to the Gospels being read or reading them for ourselves, especially when it comes to the actual words of Jesus, it is nothing less than God speaking directly to us. This is what people need to grasp again today that Christ is truly and uniquely present every time the Gospel is read and proclaimed. His very words are meant to infuse us with his life, to feed us and sustain us, to speak both to our hearts and our souls as he assures us, '**I am always with you, even to the end of time.**' (Matthew 28:20) In fact Jesus tells us quite plainly, '**Therefore, everyone who listens to these words of mine and acts on them will be like a sensible man who built his house on rock.**' (Matthew 7:24)

I am now going to repeat myself, sorry! If we are going to make any kind of progress in our understanding and appreciation of the real meaning of Easter then we need or rather we must invest some of our own time, energy and effort into the process, otherwise it simply will not work. Now nobody is going to make you do this and if it is too much to ask then you can, of course, simply stop reading right now, close this book, go away and do something else, it is entirely up to you. If you do, however, decide to read on though, with this book in one hand and your Bible, more importantly in the other, be prepared for your life to be changed forever.

Jesus once said, '**The Kingdom of Heaven is like treasure hidden in a field which someone has found; he hides it again, goes off in his joy, sells everything he owns and buys the field.**' (Matthew 13:44) Those early Christians we have spoken so much about saw the word of God like a treasure; this is something that we need to rediscover, an enthusiasm for the life transforming, life giving, word of God.

At this point I want to just stop and pause. Below you will find a list of words and phrases I have come up with which summarise what I have been trying to say so far about the importance of the Gospels, see how many of them speak to you.

'This is the Gospel, the Good News of Jesus Christ, Son of God' (Mark 1:1)

- Jesus is present and speaks to us in his word
- Jesus is alive and fills us with hope in him
- Jesus provides us with the words of eternal life
- Jesus speaks to us as the risen and glorified Lord
- Jesus's words are spirit, truth and life
- Jesus speaks to our heart and soul
- The words of Jesus make us truly alive
- The words of Jesus are timeless and speak to every age
- The words of Jesus cannot be silenced
- Jesus us invites us to build our life on his words
- The words of Jesus are unlike anything that has ever been said before

You will find throughout this book an absolute dependency on Jesus and through his word we can experience him directly as he speaks to us. This, at the same time, also allows us to **'Share in the Life of God.'** Yet the words of Jesus are also, as we shall see later, dangerous, as they are a call to action. To illustrate this we shall now explore, together, a parable told by Jesus, that makes this blatantly obvious, as a result, be prepared to be challenged!

Building on Rock (Matthew 7: 24-27)

The first point to make is that a parable is a story told by Jesus with a meaning or putting it another way, it is an earthly story with a heavenly meaning. Look now how Jesus begins this parable, **'Therefore, everyone who listens to these words of mine and acts on them, will be like a sensible man who built his house on rock.'** Notice here two things'

1. **'Everyone who listens to these words of mine'**
2. **'And acts on them.'**

This therefore means that the words of Jesus, speaking directly to us, are also a call to action! The early followers of Jesus were able to identify the link between listening to his words on the one hand and acting on them on the other. For them, as we shall discover later, everything was about continuing his presence in the world through what they said and did. To be a follower of Jesus was to be part of a community dedicated both to him and to his mission, which was to build a better world for all people. If this is ever going to be done, however, then you have to get things right from the start. So to build a house you need a firm foundation or as Jesus put it you have to build your faith on the rock of his word. Anything less than this will lead to failure, **'But everyone who listens to these words of mine and does not act on them will be like a stupid man who built his house on sand. Rain came down, floods rose, gales blew and struck that house, and it fell and what a fall it had!'**

Here then is the challenge. Are we building our lives on the rock of Jesus's words? To test this all we need do is ask of ourselves two simple questions,

1. Am I listening to the word of Jesus?
2. Am I acting on the word of Jesus?

This then leads to the most fundamental question of all, am I building the house of my life on the rock of Jesus Christ? I am not saying that other areas of faith and worship are not important but everything begins and ends with Jesus, he must be our rock of faith. It is through the Gospels that Christ speaks tenderly to us inviting us into a conversation with him. Here we listen but we are not being invited to be passive, rather as we have seen, we are being invited to act. The spirit of Christ through his word will energise us, awakening from deep within our hearts and souls something, which, perhaps, we had thought lost, his very life. When we build our lives on the rock of Christ then nothing can, in the words of Saint Paul, **'separate us from him,'** (Romans 8:39) even when times are hard because Jesus tells us, **'Rain came down, floods rose, gales blew and hurled themselves against that house, and it did not fall: it**

was founded on rock.'

The challenge for us then and indeed the church is to listen attentively to the words of Jesus and to allow them to transform our hearts, our souls and therefore our entire lives. Then we need to put those same words of life into practice by helping to build a better world. This in many ways becomes our starting point as we prepare to delve deeper into our journey in search of the real meaning of Easter. By building our lives on the rock of Christ, his words as we move ever closer to discovering the depths of his love for humanity, will speak directly to us illuminating with his Spirit all that we shall discover. Keep, therefore, his words close, revere them, respect them, cherish them but above all love them but be warned, you will be challenged to act! This is because as the word of God becomes absorbed into the fibre of our very being we suddenly realise that we are, in fact, doing nothing less than **'Sharing in the Life of God.'**

CHAPTER THREE

Meeting and Experiencing Jesus

'You're actually only really dealing with Jesus when you throw your arms around him and realise right down to the bottom of your being that this is something you can still do today.'

Karl Rahner

'Who do people say I am?' (Matthew 16: 13-16)

Perhaps, for the Christian, this question asked by Jesus to his disciples is the most important one of all. So important, in fact, that it can be found in each of the Gospels of Matthew (16: 13-16), Mark (8: 27-29) and Luke (9:18-20). I lecture in Christology, a subject, which explores the identity of Jesus, at Saint Mary's College, the seminary for the Archdiocese of Birmingham. The very first question I ask the students on the course is, 'Who is Jesus for you?' I then give them time to reflect on their answers before writing them down and then sharing them with the rest of the group. Here is how some of them, over time, have responded,

'He is my Lord and saviour.'

'He saved me from my sins and offers me new life.'

'He is my Lord and my God, my saviour and my king.'

'He died for us and loves us.'

'He is the Lamb of God, the King of Kings and Lord of Lords.'

'He is my brother, my friend and my saviour.'

'He is the redeemer and saviour of the world, the Son of God in human form.'

'He is the incarnate Son of God who came to save us from sin and give us new life.'

I then set them a task to prepare a homily to preach to their own congregations on this very question but before they can do this, they really need to reflect, at a deeper and more personal level, on what the question is really asking of them.

At this point let us go back to Jesus. He has been teaching in and around the foothills of Galilee for some time an area he knows well because he grew up there. He has kept to the small towns and villages focusing much of his attention on the poor, downtrodden and outcast. The disciples have witnessed the miracles and heard Jesus teach and preach in ways that had never been heard of or seen before. In addition to this they had been so inspired by him that they had literally dropped everything including their wives, families and livelihoods to follow him. Then Jesus takes them to one side and simply asks them the question, **'Who do people say I am?'** They then replied, **'Some say John the Baptist; others Elijah; and still others, Jeremiah or one of the Prophets.'** (Matthew 16:14) Or in other words the people are confused they are not quite sure who you are. So Jesus comes back at them by asking, **'Who do you say that I am?'** (Matthew 16:15) At this point I get the impression that there was one of those long awkward silences when nobody says anything because no one is quite sure what to say. In the end it is Peter who bursts out, **'You are the Christ, the Son of the living God.'** A little later Jesus then predicts that he must go to Jerusalem where he will suffer and die. At this point Peter takes him to one side and says, **'God forbid, Lord. Such a fate must never happen to you.'** (Matthew 16:22) Jesus then says to Peter, **'Get behind me, Satan! You are an obstacle to me. You are thinking not as God does, but as men do.'** (Matthew 16:23)

What are we to make of this remarkable encounter so important that it is included in all three of the Synoptic Gospels? Perhaps the first point to make is to ask the question, did Peter really know what he was saying when he said to Jesus, **'You are the Christ, the Son of the living God?'** Did he know that such a Christ would have to suffer and die to reveal the true nature of God? Apparently not or else why did he try to persuade Jesus from his course? Secondly although he may have meant what he said when he identified Jesus as the Christ did he really understand it? Once again the evidence suggests that he did not. So what was going on inside of Peter when he made his proclamation of faith?

Returning to my students at the seminary what I want them to do first and foremost is to answer the question for themselves but from the inside. I am not looking for a doctrinal answer, which does not touch the heart but for one, which reveals a close and personal relationship with the living Lord. Only then can they offer something to those outside of themselves, that is to say the people to whom they are ministering. What this calls for is a close examination of our own answer to the question, which Jesus asks of us, **'Who do you say I am?'** So how about this then as a proposal? What if Jesus is really asking the question not about him but about us? Who do we really believe in? In whom do we really place all our hope and all our trust? What, therefore, is the heart, the centre and the focus of what we really believe in, for whom do we really live our lives? To answer this question we need, at least for a while, to turn away from doctrinal formulas and look at what we really believe in and how this inspires us to actually live our lives. To do this, however, we have to start from the inside and work outwards.

So where do we start? First we have to begin our journey from within and accept that following Jesus is nothing less than dangerous. Look at it like this and let us be honest with ourselves here, after all who are we trying to kid, only ourselves. So most of us are selfish, motivated by self-interest, fact! Now let us look at Jesus and what do we find, the opposite. Jesus is selfless, always interested first and foremost in the needs of others, especially those who are rejected, despised, unwanted and unloved. Reflect, if you will, on his compassion, tenderness, mercy, justice and above all love. Compare that to our values and what happens? Next reflect on Jesus's intimate relationship with his Father, one in which he invites us to share. This is the Jesus we need to know from the inside out if we are ever going to answer his question, **'Who am I?'** But to do this has to involve a revolution within our own hearts because we have to literally become tender-hearted, just like him. Equally and at the same time we have to develop through him an intimate and personal relationship with God, which ultimately can be seen in action through our deeds of mercy, compassion, forgiveness and love in the world in which we live. Or in other words by and through God's grace our inner lives have to be so transformed by our relationship with Jesus that we actually become living flames of his love so that in our actions others can tangibly see what it means to live lives of selfless love.

Now let us go back to Peter and his response to the question posed by Jesus, **'Who do people say I am?'** Peter says, **'You are the Christ, the Son of the living God,'** but all too soon demonstrates that he clearly does not know what this means. It would, in fact, take Peter many years and many mistakes for him to comprehend the full meaning of what he said. In that time he would fail to recognise Jesus as the servant of God when he refused to have his feet washed by him at the end of the last supper. He along with James and John would fail to stay awake with Jesus, as he prayed in the garden of

Gethsemane, the night before his death. Again Peter along with all the other disciples would desert Jesus when the guards sent by the high priest came to arrest him. Equally it would be Peter who when questioned by the servants in the courtyard, as Jesus was being interrogated by Caiaphas, denied ever having known him three times. Peter would not be present at the foot of the cross nor would he believe the women who told him about the resurrection, instead he insisted on seeing the empty tomb for himself. Then finally after seeing the resurrected Jesus Peter simply went back to his old way of life, that of being a fisherman.

It would, in fact, take a long time, much reflection and soul searching, for Peter to undergo an inner transformation by God's grace and through the imparting of the Holy Spirit, before he fully comprehended what it actually meant to call Jesus, **'The Christ, the Son of the living God.'** But once that happened, once his heart had been touched, once enlightened by grace he looked back at his life with Jesus and that was when everything changed for him. At this point his transformation on the inside was testified to by his actions on the outside and this is exactly what I am saying applies to us too. Everything comes back to our relationship with Christ and what that means through a lived experience, which can be seen in action. This, in turn, now brings us right back to my earlier premise that Jesus through asking this question is really making it about us. In other words it is nothing less than a call to action by Jesus because recognition of him cannot be separated from how we live. Or putting it another way the Christian life, which through grace, given by God, enables us to recognise Jesus as the Christ, the Son of the living God, cannot be divorced from the way we are invited to live.

In the early days of Christianity Jesus stood at the heart of everything and so it was vitally important for those first Christians to not only know who Jesus was but also what he was inviting them to do. Going back to my students at the seminary it is fairly easy to define Jesus by way of a formula we learnt many years ago and have recited ever since but does this touch our hearts and transform our lives from the inside out? Instead, perhaps, we need to reflect more deeply on the person of Jesus himself because the Christian faith is not founded on doctrine or dogma put on a person, Jesus Christ. Sometimes out of shear familiarity we tend to forget the radical and revolutionary nature of the God who breaks into our lives in and through his Son. To understand this we need to reflect more deeply on the uniqueness of his life and let him touch our hearts and lives from the inside. Staggeringly this God invites us to participate with him in a mission to love the world, **'For God so loved the world that he gave his only Son.'** (John 3:16) Such love, however, has to be experienced on the inside first before it can be lived on the outside.

As I remarked earlier for those early Christians Jesus was at the heart of their lives giving meaning to everything they did. We too are called to live our lives like that, to be motivated by what motivated him, to serve just like him, to be merciful just like him, to forgive just like him, to be compassionate just like him and, of course, to love just like him. Now this can only be achieved when faith is experienced and lived from the inside out when the spirit of Jesus himself feeds our very lives. If then, as I proposed earlier, Jesus is really asking the question of us as to **'Who am I?'** The only authentic answer is one that is reflected in not only what we say but also by what we do.

The very essence of Christianity is to be found in Jesus, if we forget or abandon this we become lost. If we drift too far away from Jesus again we become lost. It is the reason why the world, increasingly, is failing to understand Christianity but has little problem in highlighting the importance of social justice. For the Christian Jesus gives meaning to life but if this is to be fully grasped, let alone lived, then he must be encountered and experienced personally but again from the inside. Many people in the world today are becoming increasingly dissatisfied with any systems, which fall foul to corruption, insincerity, hedonism and selfishness. Instead people crave honesty, integrity, decency and justice all of which can be found in Jesus Christ. Most people, I would suggest, get this and admire Jesus but they do not experience him in ways that they can understand and comprehend. What they do know with certainty, however, is that they will reject any institutionalised version of Christianity, which preaches one thing but does another. This only serves to highlight the vital importance of Christians living authentic lives, which in and of themselves point to the values of Jesus because they were actually lived by him. Anything less than this fails to inspire others for whom Jesus is nothing less than a distant memory of a good man.

The fundamental premise of this chapter is that the calling to Christianity, which is nothing less than an invitation by Christ himself, is something which must first and foremost touch our hearts on the inside. It is literally about being seduced by Jesus and falling in love with him to the point that he motivates everything that we do. Only when this happens can our lives be so enlivened by him, so transformed by him that we can actually see that he calls us to participate in his very life by how we live our lives on the outside. This is what living a life of faith, the source of which is nothing less than Christ himself, actually means. Only lives lived in this way will draw others to the God who, unconditionally and literally, loves all people.

Finally there is something else to add which takes us deeper into understanding our relationship with Jesus and what this means for living an authentic Christian life. The main focus of this chapter has been on highlighting the importance of having an inner experience of Jesus, which results in a deeper personal relationship with him. Yet there will be aspects of this relationship, which by its very nature will differ from person to person in its uniqueness. However, the values of Jesus, which correspond to the values of the Kingdom of Heaven, remain constant. For in him is revealed, for all people, the God of mercy, compassion, forgiveness, justice and love. These must be the values of the Christian too. For in him is revealed also the love of God for the poor, rejected, abandoned, despised, unwanted, wretched and unloved. These, therefore, must equally be the values of anyone who would walk in the footsteps of Christ. It is sad to think that many or dare I say most people do not know or recognise who this Jesus actually is but this becomes worse if and when it actually applies to Christians.

So now we can go right back to the beginning when it appeared that Jesus was asking a question about himself when in fact, all along, he was asking a question about you and me.

Some additional comments

Education

I have decided to add something here that I was not going to include but do not feel right ignoring. I have spent most of my adult life in education across the complete age range from very young children at one end right up to and including adults at the other. If Religious Education in our faith schools does not attempt to help young people develop a close and personal, lived and experienced relationship with Jesus, as I have outlined in this chapter, then it is, in my opinion, doing the young people entrusted to their care a serious disservice. Sometimes all of us need to be brave enough to ask ourselves the question, 'Do I actually recognise who Jesus is?' Imagine then if the very structures and systems we have created, with the very best of intentions, actually prevent our young people from recognising who Jesus really is, so that for them, just like for most people, he becomes, eventually, an irrelevance. Shocking I know but could it be true? Next time you are in church take a good look around you and ask yourself, 'Where are all the young people?' Perhaps they are not there because they have drifted away from the God they never really knew or because they feel disillusioned by a church which tells people to do one thing but does the opposite itself. Yet I bet that you do not have to look too far from finding such young people passionately involved in projects focusing on social justice, the environment and making the world in which we live a better place for all people. Sounds familiar? Of course it does because this is exactly what Jesus did when he revealed the values of the Kingdom of Heaven.

So what then is the answer? You cannot identify the problem without offering some sort of solution, surely! Well I would say this, instead of being obsessed with examination grades, results and league tables instead be passionate about what motivated Jesus; fairness, equality, justice, mercy, compassion, forgiveness and above all else love but for all people. Help our young to know Christ first, to fall in love with him, to be seduced by him, to be transformed by him. Or, in other words, to find Christ on the inside of their own lives so that their relationship with him becomes a personal and experienced one. Then enable them to discover what this actually means for living life on the outside by being committed to participating in his mission for the salvation of the whole world. If our young people (here I really mean all of us by the way) could grasp what God is actually inviting us to do and to be, nothing less than participate in his very life, then all our lives would be transformed and the world could not help but take notice. However, the most radical part of this proposal is that a life of faith, lived according to the values of Jesus, is one to be shared through acts of love for all people where everyone is included and no one is excluded. New? No, because that was exactly what Jesus said and did!

Coronavirus 2020

One final thing before I end this chapter. At the moment I am writing this in the midst of the Coronavirus – COVID-19. The situation across the world is terrible with thousands of people being contaminated and many of them dying alone, in isolation, separated from loved ones, some of whom cannot even attend their funerals. It's like the whole world is suffering and it brings my attention back to the very first chapter in this book, which I wrote before any of this happened. In it, you may recall, that I identified suffering as the key to understanding everything, especially when it comes to our response to it. Now here is the thing and it applies across the world and it cannot be denied that what we are seeing right before our very eyes is a response to suffering. Here I am talking about the doctors, nurses, carers and all medical staff along with all those key workers who are literally putting their own lives on the line, every day, by responding to the suffering of others. On the news we see exhausted doctors and nurses time and time again going back to what is being called the front line and literally, once again, before our very eyes doing whatever they can to relieve the pain, misery and suffering of others. It is exhausting, brutal and emotionally draining work and yet across the world these people carry on. In many places, including the UK, people have recognised this and have arranged for organised outbursts of applause to take place in recognition of and in gratitude for all their hard work and commitment. People's hearts have been touched on the inside giving rise to expressing how they feel on the outside through these organised events. Other people have donated food, whilst some have offered transport alongside similar kind acts of simple gratitude.

For me I would humbly suggest that in the selfless acts of the medical staff and all those called to serve others in these moments of extreme crisis, I see nothing less than the actions of Christ himself who came, **'Not to be served but to serve.'** (Matthew 20:28) I think, personally, that people get this, perhaps not in the way I have articulated it here but they do get it. You see when it comes down to it, people's hearts have been touched by the selfless service and love of others to the point whereby they need to respond or express their gratitude in some external way, so that which has been experienced on the inside finds expression on the outside. Perhaps when this crisis is over the world will change and we will all be more willing to accept that how we respond to suffering is the very key to understanding how to be a human being. I will now, finally, conclude this chapter by humbly proposing that this is exactly what Jesus came to reveal, proclaim and live out, over 2,000 years ago.

CHAPTER FOUR

Lent

'Come, Follow Me' (Matthew 4:19)

Matthew 4: 1-11

Some people may well be tempted to ask the question in a book about Easter why are you writing about Lent? The answer to this is and putting it quite simply that preparation is, in fact, everything. The Christian faith is essentially about transformation or putting it another way it is about a total change in our lives. There is a wonderful word in Greek, the original language of the New Testament, 'Metanoia,' which means a complete change of heart or a spiritual conversion. Indeed, this is what Jesus is calling for when he utters his first words in the Gospels, **'Repent for the Kingdom of Heaven is near.'** (Matthew 3:2). I have a great amount of respect for the late great biblical scholar Raymond E Brown. One of the stories I love about him is that very often he would turn up to his lectures and deliver them without any notes. He would do the same for any talks, homilies or speeches that he was invited to give. However, some people criticised him for his apparent arrogance. So to combat this he took up the practice of taking his brief case with him giving the impression it contained his notes when instead all

43

that it contained was his lunch! The moral of this story is that it took Raymond E Brown all his life, a life of work, prayer and constant study and reflection for him to arrive, before his audience, to deliver a talk on God's word. This was something, in fact, that he never took for granted; moreover he saw it as a huge privilege. Yet thorough and prolonged preparation was the foundation of everything he did.

It takes a doctor in excess of five years to qualify, whilst for those studying for the priesthood it can take up to seven. Preparation then is vitally important but before we proceed to focus some attention on ourselves it is crucial to recognise that before Jesus began his teaching and preaching ministry he entered into a period of prolonged preparation. In the early days of Christianity candidates for baptism would often spend up to a year preparing to be received into the church at Easter. Scholars have even worked out that it took Saint Paul up to three years, after his conversion to Christ, before he really understood what God was asking him to do next. If we recognise the importance of preparation in certain key areas of life, then we need to do the same when it comes to our relationship with God. In other words it requires us to put in some time, energy and effort, which will not lead to commercial benefit but it may well lead to the transformation of our whole life. I think we have lost something of this in the life of the church today where we have become almost too frightened to ask people to invest their time in their faith. Jesus in his teaching and preaching ministry constantly challenged people, confronting them with the **Kingdom of Heaven.**

Some of them found the challenge too much and they fell away but that did not mean that Jesus stopped loving them. What it did mean, however, was that there would be a price or a cost to discipleship. There is that wonderful scene in John's Gospel where Jesus has been teaching the people about the meaning of who he is, **'I am the bread of life,'** (John 6:48) he says, **'Whoever eats my flesh and drinks my blood lives in me and I in him.'** (John 6:56) At this point we are told, **'many of his disciples turned away and no longer remained with him.'** (John 6: 66) Now Jesus turns to the twelve and asks, **'Do you also wish to leave?'** (6:67) in other words he is laying down a challenge or at least the option for them to go and leave him. It is, in fact, Peter who answers, **'Lord, to whom shall we go? You have the words of eternal life.'** (John 6:68)

In the same way Jesus lays down a challenge to us. You do not have to read this book, you can in fact, stop now; you do not have to go on, that is your choice. However, if you do decide to proceed you will be asked to do something because that is how it works. You must be prepared to have your life transformed not by reading this book, of course, but by God's grace. Hopefully reading this book will be part of that process. It has taken me a life-time of prayer, study and reflection to reach this point and I believe it is nothing less than God's grace that has lead me here. So we are embarking on a journey together, holding each other's hands so to speak but recognising that it will cost us that we will change and never be the same again. When Peter spoke to Jesus on behalf of all the disciples he said, **'We have come to believe and know that you are the Holy One of God.'** (John 6:68) This is our starting point too. Jesus holds out his hand to us and says, **'Come, follow me.'** (Matthew 4:19) What we have to do now is have the courage to take his hand in our own and see where he leads us.

Our preparation for Easter will begin with Jesus in the wilderness. (Matthew 4:1-11) It is important to note that; **'Jesus was led by the Spirit into the desert,'** where he would be without food for forty days and forty nights. It is safe for us to assume therefore, at this point, that he would have been hungry and exhausted, which left him open to temptation. We too need to recognise that we are constantly open to temptation, to be distracted and to be drawn away from God's invitation to, **'Come, follow me.'** There will, as we all know, appear to be those things in life which are more important, more essential, and even more vital to us than accepting the invitation of Jesus to, **'Come, follow me.'** The first thing we need to do is just to be aware of them, to recognise and accept them, for what they are, attempts to persuade us that there are more important things in life than discipleship.

In our Gospel reading (Matthew 4: 1-11) Satan comes to Jesus and attempts to do just that. You see he recognises something vitally important that if, somehow, he can distract Jesus from his relationship with his Father then his ministry will be over before it begins. Seeing that Jesus is hungry he starts with the sarcastic refrain, **'If you are the Son of God, tell these stones to become**

bread.' At the heart of this temptation is the attempt by Satan to undermine Jesus's entire ministry at the heart of which is his relationship with his Father. So will Jesus put his own self-interest first? Will he turn stones into bread to satisfy his own hunger? This is the most fundamental question of all and attacks Jesus at the core of his being, 'is he or will he be the man for others?' Jesus will be the one who, in fact, in his ministry goes out to, identifies, and feeds the hungry, something so important it is found in all four gospels. (Matthew 14: 13-21; Mark 6: 31-44; Luke: 9:12-17; John 6:1-14) Moreover, Jesus's nourishment, which will sustain him throughout his ministry, will be the living word of God. Hence his reply to Satan becomes, '**Man does not live on bread alone, but on every word that comes from the mouth of God.'**

We now need to apply this to ourselves. How often are, in life, motivated by self-interest? This is a serious question and requires honesty and careful reflection. Perhaps at this point we actually need to stop reading and make a concerted effort to be with Jesus in our own wilderness and take the time to write things down, if it would help, as to what really motivates us in life. Where do our real priorities lie? How much of what we do and say actually pushes us further away from God? Now, however, we know what to do and it is to put, as far as possible, self-interest to one side and make a conscious decision to place the needs of other people before our own. Give yourself some time, come back when you are ready and remember that this is all part of our preparation for Easter.

Just before we leave the first temptation it is important for us to note that Jesus throughout his entire ministry put the needs of others, especially the poor, the rejected, the despised, the unwanted and the unloved constantly before his own needs. Imagine what the Church would look like if it did the opposite to this. What would our discipleship look like if we did the opposite to this? An authentic Church and authentic discipleship cannot and should not be motivated by self-interest. Would it be too much to say, therefore, that whenever or wherever either the Church, or its members, put self-interest first, it is being unfaithful to Jesus? Having identified our first temptation as self-interest and by making a concerted effort to put this to one side we can now move on to the second temptation. But before we do this this let us make one final point.

Putting others before self is the way of Christ. Whenever, we practice this same virtue we are doing nothing less than, 'Sharing in the life of God.' This then becomes our first step, our first challenge even, in preparing for Easter and we shall call it the way of selfless love. As we journey through the season of Lent we need to constantly look for ways of how to practice putting the needs of others before our own.

We can now proceed to explore the second temptation of Jesus, which takes place at the Temple, in Jerusalem. Once again Satan begins with a sarcastic refrain, **'If you are the Son of God,'** he said, **'throw yourself down; for scripture says: He has given his angels orders about you, and they will carry you in their arms in case**

you trip over a stone.' (Matthew 4: 5-6; Psalm 91: 10-12)

So what exactly is going on here and how can we apply it to our own lives today as part of our preparation for Easter? Matthew, in fact, tells us that Jesus is taken, by Satan, to the very top or parapet of the Temple and invited to throw himself off. 'Surely God, your Father, will save you by sending his angels,' we can almost hear him say. Here what Satan is doing is to invite Jesus to be that which he is not, a glorious Messiah. 'Show people how important you are, how magnificent you are, go on show people what you can do as the Son of God, let everyone see and believe in you through your miraculous powers. You have nothing to fear, have you? After all, surely your Father will not allow you to be hurt and you do have total faith in him, do you not?' What we are seeing here is, once again, an attempt by Satan to undermine Jesus's relationship with his Father. Jesus, of course, sees through this straight away and so immediately responds, **'Do no put the Lord your God to the test**.' In other words Jesus will not be a glorious Messiah and refuses to put God, his heavenly Father, at his own vain service. Rather he has come as, **'one who serves, not to be served.'** (Luke 22:27) Jesus therefore refuses to do anything, which will glorify himself. Jesus refuses to perform signs or miracles except for when they will relieve the pain, misery and suffering of others. Any such signs will instead, in and of themselves, assure people of his Father's mercy, compassion, forgiveness and love, whilst at the same time glorifying God in heaven.

What now can we learn from this and so put into practice in our own lives as we prepare for Easter? One of the main criteria, if I can use that term, for following Jesus is to seek only to do good. Such goodness, following the example of Jesus, is to seek to help those in need and rather than give glory to us, to give glory to God. Jesus makes a big deal of doing such things in secret, **'But when you give alms, your left hand must not know what your right is doing; your almsgiving must be secret, and your Father who sees all that is done in secret will reward you.'** (Matthew 6:4) The second criteria, again following the example of Jesus, is to act as a servant, **'Yet here am I among you as one who serves!'** (Luke 22:27) In other words to be a follower of Jesus there must be no attempt at self-aggrandisement, to make ourselves more important or more special than anyone else. No! Instead we should simply attempt to do two things:

- Only do good
- Act as a servant

So would it be too much to say that whenever or wherever the Church or its members seeks to put its own glory before God, it is being unfaithful to Jesus? The Church and its members are invited by Christ to be servants of God in the world by doing only good but this must be done in and through loving service, there is and can be no other way. This is made perfectly clear in the life and teachings of Jesus himself. This is because it is this loving service, which will lead Jesus, ultimately, to the cross, but it is also this loving service that will transform the world.

Perhaps now we are beginning to understand the second part of our preparation for Easter. This time Jesus is inviting us to be humble servants at the service of others by doing only good. Equally our actions are not to be done in order to draw attention to ourselves, rather they are to be carried out in secret and any glory involved is to be given to God. Give yourselves, now, some time to decide how you might go about this. What good actions could you perform for others as a servant of God's mercy, compassion, forgiveness and love? Once again, to respond to this call to action by Christ himself is nothing less than participation or a 'Sharing in the Life of God.'

We can now move on to the final temptation of Jesus, which in many ways is the greatest one of all. This time Jesus is taken to the top of a high mountain and shown all the kingdoms of the world, which appear to be under the control of Satan himself. At this point Jesus is made a most incredible offer, **'I will give you all these,'** he tells him but there is one condition, **'if you fall at my feet and do me homage.'** This time Jesus's response is immediate and vehement, **'Away with you Satan! For scripture says, The Lord your God is the one to whom you must do homage, him alone must you serve.'** (Matthew 4:10; Deuteronomy 6:13)

What now are we to make of this? Jesus surveys the kingdoms of the world, the whole of humanity and almost snaps back at Satan in anger! In truth and as we have already seen Jesus has come as the servant of God not to control, dominate or manipulate but to serve all those who live on the margins of society. At the same time this also reveals the very nature and being of God. You see God never forces, nor does he seek to dominate, manipulate or control, rather, in him, as we have already seen there is only mercy, compassion, forgiveness and love. The Devil, however, represents and desires the opposite of this and knows all too well that we are susceptible to such temptations. After all imagine how you might respond if you were, literally, offered anything you wanted, without any limits being attached. The Kingdom of God, however, takes the values of the world and turns them upside down. If the world values status, power, control and wealth, the Kingdom of God does not. Indeed, God will not impose his Kingdom on the world at all, instead he offers and I use that word quite intentionally, only the gift of his love given freely through his Son, **'For this is how much God loved the world: that he gave his only Son.'** (John 3:16)

If then we are to accept Jesus's invitation to, **'Come, follow me,'** we too need to resist all attempts to be seduced by the desire to control, manipulate and dominate others. We too need to resist any obsession with status, ambition and wealth. Would it be too much to say, therefore, that whenever or wherever the Church or its members seek to use power, manipulation or domination to control others it is, in fact, being unfaithful to Jesus? There is much to think about and reflect upon here for all of us. Perhaps at this point we should pause, again, and gently review our own lives. Where do our true priorities lie? Do we really want to change and be transformed by a love beyond our understanding and the comprehension of the world in which we live? Do we really want to accept Christ's invitation to be his disciple in the world today and to make a difference, especially to all those living on the margins of society? These are the things God challenges us with. These are the issues we cannot escape if we are to truly understand the real meaning of Easter.

If then we are to prepare effectively for Easter we need to put to one side any cravings we might have which seek to control others, any obsessions we might have with wealth, ambition or power and replace them with the humble love of God. It is the love of God, which must dominate our lives and transform our souls because to love like him is to do nothing less than to participate and therefore 'Share in the life of God' himself.

Summary

We are making a journey into the real meaning of Easter but if we are to get anywhere near understanding this high point of the church's year then our hearts and minds have to be transformed. This can only happen by and through God's grace, we cannot do it by ourselves. If this is to happen, however, the first step we have to take is to be open to it. That is to say we have to open our hearts and minds to God's grace and see what happens. Yet we are not required to be passive, in fact the reverse is true because as we pointed out right at the beginning of this chapter, preparation is everything and this is where Lent comes in. Lent gives us forty days to get ourselves ready for Easter and our first step is to go out into our own wilderness with Jesus by our side.

The next thing to acknowledge is that we will be challenged by God to do something. In other words Jesus's invitation to follow him is a call to action. As a result we identified three characteristics of discipleship each linked to the three temptations of Jesus in the wilderness. These can be summarised as follows:

1. *We must put self-interest to one side and instead focus our attention on the needs of others. This is the way of the selfless love of Christ.*
2. *To seek, as God's servant, only to do what is good.*
3. *To be dominated not by power, wealth and ambition but only by the love of God as revealed in his Son, Jesus Christ.*

Each of these in their own way, as we have seen, when practiced, allow us to '**Share in the Life of God.**' That is a very powerful thing to say but it is true. Yet we are only just starting out on our journey and there is still much more to come but everything is totally dependent on the resurrection of Jesus. This is how Saint Paul put it, '**If there is no resurrection of the dead, then Christ cannot have been raised either and if Christ has not been raised, then our preaching is without substance, and so is our faith.**' (1 Corinthians 15: 13-14) Everything then and by that I mean the entire

Christian faith rests on Christ's resurrection from the dead, that is the real meaning of Easter and this is where our journey into its truth begins.

CHAPTER FIVE

Palm (Passion) Sunday

'It is no longer I who live but it is Christ who lives in me'

(Galatians 2:20)

Matthew 26: 14-27: 66

With Psalm or Passion Sunday we enter what Christians call **'Holy Week'** and as such God offers to us an invitation, one that has been there, in fact, for the whole of our lives and that is simply this, 'Join me.'

This week is like no other because it will literally lead to the transformation of everything including time and the whole of creation. Saint Paul put it like this, **'Consequently, anyone united to Christ is a new creation. The old order has passed away. Behold, all has become new.'** (2 Corinthians 5:17) However, for all of this to happen God in and through his Son, Jesus Christ, must die. Or putting it another way God will recreate everything but he will do so from the inside out. To achieve this, however, he would become one of us, he would become one with us, **'For the word** became flesh and dwelt among us,' (John 1:14), and 'they shall call him Emmanuel, a name which means, "God is with us."' (Matthew 1:23) Only by being one of us and by being one with us will God do what we were incapable of doing and that is defeat and destroy the three great enemies of humanity, Satan, Sin and Death. It is this same God who invites us to follow him as we enter the final stages of his Son's mission on earth.

However, before we accept such an invitation we need first of all to pause and reflect, as far as that is possible, on what it actually means. Jesus himself makes it very clear that, **'Anyone who wishes to be a follower of mine must deny himself, take up his cross and follow me. For whoever wishes to save his life will lose it, but whoever loses his life for my sake will find it.'** (Matthew 16: 24-25) To accept the invitation given to us by Jesus then in his mission to transform and therefore recreate everything will cost us our very lives! It certainly will not be easy, the price will be high and everything will change but there is and cannot be any other way. The question now is, knowing this will we still accept his invitation. Once a rich young man asked Jesus how to inherit eternal life? After quoting the commandments the rich young man was then challenged by Jesus to, **'Sell everything you own, give your money to the poor and you will have treasure in heaven. Then come, follow me.'** (Luke 18:18-26) At that point the rich young man knew that Jesus was, in fact, asking him to do the one thing he could not do. However, if we are tempted to lose heart at this point Jesus offers us consolation by telling us, **'For God all things are possible.'** (Matthew 19:26)

Yet what is clear is that to accept Jesus's invitation to follow him is to step out of the darkness and into the light and respond to his call for action. Christianity is not and can never be reduced to a merely intellectual exercise. Rather it is a call to join Jesus in his mission, which is nothing less than the transformation of the whole world, including us, and that if we accept his invitation there can be no turning back, **'No one who puts his hand to the plough and then looks back is fit for the kingdom of God.'** (Luke 9:62) If we are to follow in the footsteps of Jesus then we need to know and understand, as far as that is possible, what, in fact, we are committing ourselves to, which is nothing less than making the world, in which we live, a better place, for all people. If we can do this we are beginning to recognise and understand what it means to be a human being, which is something that in its totality only God, in and through his Son, can teach us.

Accepting the invitation of Jesus then is to join with him and therefore to participate in the very life of God by attempting to establish his Kingdom on earth. The very first words of Jesus in the Gospels are, **'Repent for the Kingdom of God is at hand.'** (Matthew 3:2, Mark 1:15) Discipleship, therefore, is not only to share in this vision but to help realise it in the here and now. But what does this mean? Quite simply, it means to become living flames of God's love in the world by bringing,

- *Love where there was only hate*
- *Forgiveness where there was only thirst for revenge*
- *Truth where there was only lies*
- *Compassion where there was only indifference*
- *Mercy where there was only hard-heartedness*
- *Justice where there was only unfairness*

With this comes an understanding that the God of Jesus Christ is the God of mercy, compassion, forgiveness and love and it is he who invites us to bind ourselves to him in his mission to save the world. Now we can begin to understand our role in the world, which is to live according to the values of the Kingdom of Heaven. To achieve this then we need to build that Kingdom up in our own hearts, in our own lives and in the communities we belong to. With Christ at the very centre of our lives and of our communities we can look to his spirit to animate us into action.

Yet we cannot escape the fact that this decision to follow Jesus will inevitably, as it did for him, lead to conflict, pain, humiliation and suffering, **'Then you will be handed over to be tortured and put to death and you will be hated by all nations because of my name.'** (Matthew 24:9) At this point we may well ask ourselves, why? Why would people resist such efforts to make the world in which we live a better place for all people? The kind of world revealed as the will of God by Jesus is a more loving world, a more just world and ultimately a more human world. Jesus, in fact, reveals and realises in himself the potential for the human race, so why would anyone not want that? Or putting it another way, if what Jesus teaches and reveals about making the world a better place for all people is not what is wanted, then what kind of world do people desire?

As Jesus enters Jerusalem then he brings the Gospel, the Good News, of the Kingdom of Heaven with him, it is this same Good News, which compels his followers today into action by,

- **Feeding the hungry**
- **Giving the thirsty something to drink**
- **Welcoming the stranger**
- **Clothing the naked**
- **Taking care of the sick**
- **Visiting those in prison (Matthew 25: 35-36)**

Perhaps the crowds of people who had gathered together to greet him had heard of the miracles he had performed and of the Good News he proclaimed. Perhaps too they sensed that a change was immanent, that God was going to act again, as he did in the days of old and that at last they would be freed from the captivity of Roman rule. Hence, we are told, **'and the crowds that went before him and that followed him shouted, "Hosanna to the Son of David! Hosanna in the highest!" And when he entered Jerusalem, all the city was stirred, saying, "Who is this?" And the crowds said, "This is the prophet Jesus from Nazareth of Galilee."** (Matthew 21:9-11)

Yet all too soon those same crowds of people were shouting, **'Let him be crucified!'** (Matthew 27:22) The fundamental question is, of course, why? Why did the crowd appear to change their minds about Jesus? Yet we do not have to look very far for the answer. Once Jesus became a threat to Caiaphas the high priest and the priestly aristocracy he represented, the fate of Jesus was in fact sealed, this is because they held a privileged status given to them by their Roman masters. Their brief was simple, in exchange for the office they held which brought with it all kinds of financial and property based privileges; all they had to do was make sure that the people kept the peace. The minute Jesus became a threat to this, due to his popularity with the people, he had to be dealt with, and after all **'it is better for us that one man die for the people than the whole nation be destroyed.'** (John 11:50) One vital contribution towards this was when Jesus condemned the actions of those making financial profit in the Temple by overturning the tables of the money changers and saying, **'It is written: "My house shall be called a house of prayer, but you are making it a den of thieves."** (Matthew 21:13) What we are, in fact, witnessing here is nothing less than a clash between two ways of looking at the world and therefore life. On the one hand you have Jesus and the values of the Kingdom of Heaven, which put the weak, despised, crushed, forgotten, voiceless and poor at the centre of everything. Whilst on the other hand you have the values of the world, which put power, wealth, privilege and status above all other things. When the former threatens the latter it leads to annihilation, just look at history.

As we said earlier Jesus invites us to join him, to walk in his footsteps, to participate in his mission for the salvation of the world but it will not be easy. To take the side of those on the margins, to be the voice for the voiceless, to be there for the weak and powerless and to assure them of God's love is what Jesus asks us to do if we would follow him. We will be persecuted, we will be rejected, we will be called all kinds of things and there will be no guarantee of protection or security apart from his all-redeeming love. This is because ultimately, what makes present the Kingdom of God is his saving justice, peace and joy, which can only be brought about by the Holy Spirit. (Romans 14:17)

Perhaps at this point we need to stop and ask ourselves, 'what kind of world do we really want to live in and what are we prepared to do to achieve it?' Jesus revealed, as we have already seen, in and through his life and ministry, the values of the Kingdom of Heaven. At the same time he makes no attempt to deceive us because the decision to follow Jesus will involve a cross for each and every single one of us. This cross, which we are required to take up if we are follow him, will involve pain, persecution, humiliation and suffering. If we cannot accept this then we must stop now. There is no compulsion, at all, to follow his fate; it is by its very nature an invitation, which to the world appears madness, **'For the foolishness of God is wiser than human wisdom, and the weakness of God is stronger than human strength.'** (1 Corinthians 1:25) Yet this is what discipleship is and it cannot be entered into half-heartedly, perhaps this is why many people today just do not get it. We cannot nor should we reduce discipleship to something, which ranks low in our list of priorities. We cannot teach or give the impression that discipleship involves compromise, that it does not really matter, that serving and loving Christ in the poor and the needy is some kind of add on to normal life! Rather the Church needs to rediscover the energy of Jesus, that it has a precious treasure to offer the world and that through the Gospel everything can be transformed. However, as I have already laboured to point out it will not be easy and we should not pretend that it is, after all it cost Jesus his life. There are as we know, I am sure, easier ways to live our lives but the voice of God in Christ cannot be silenced, **'enter through the narrow gate,'** (Matthew 7:13) **'Lord, allow me to go first and bury my father. Jesus answered him, Follow me, and let the dead bury their own dead.'** (Matthew 8:21-22) **'Be like the wise man who built his house on rock.'** (Matthew 7:25) In other words sitting on the fence is not an option. People will not be attracted to a lukewarm or half-hearted Gospel, because this is not the Gospel of Jesus Christ.

No! To follow Jesus is to be filled with his Spirit for life and to participate, that is to say share, in his mission to transform the world, which is nothing less than helping the human race to realise its own potential. This is the Gospel of the Lord and this is what the Church is called both to live and proclaim. Jesus stands before each and every single one of us and issues the invitation, **'Come follow me.'**

(Matthew 4:19) At first sight the invitation and task, which lies ahead of us may appear to be daunting, perhaps too much to bare but strangely and paradoxically when we accept it something wonderful and unbelievable happens, we discover that the burden is actually light because we never carry it alone.

'**Take my yoke upon you and learn from me, for I am gentle and humble of heart; and you will find rest. For my yoke is easy and my burden light.**' (Matthew 11:25-30)

Then we come to another realisation, '**It is no longer I who live, but it is Christ who lives in me.**' (Galatians 2:20)

You see the fundamental realisation of our faith is that we are in fact never alone, '**I am with you always, to the end of the world.**' (Matthew 28:20)

This concludes our first step into Holy Week as we continue our journey with Jesus deeper into in his life saving actions, which will ultimately transform everything and make all things new. There is much now, however, for us to think about and at this point I would encourage all of us to take the time and reflect on the meaning of our own call to discipleship before we move deeper into Christ's invitation to know, love and serve him by and through the love and service we offer to one another.

CHAPTER SIX

Maundy Thursday

Sharing in the Life of God

'I have given you an example so that you may copy what I have done to you.'

John 13: 1-15

There are three important points I want to make in this chapter. The first will focus on the 'Passover Meal' and how the Jewish people, to this day, believe that a life of faith is nothing less than participation or a sharing in the life of God. The second, will draw our attention to 'Holy Communion' and how this, for Christians is one of the ways God shares his life with us. The final point will draw our attention to the actions of Jesus, as described in the Gospel of John, at the last supper, when he washed the feet of his disciples, so setting an example for all people to follow. Each of these points will, in their own right, set out clearly how they allow humanity to do nothing less than share in the life of God himself.

The Passover Meal

On Maundy Thursday we hear from the book of Exodus 12: 1-8, 11-14, instructions on how the Jews are to celebrate the Passover Meal. The section ends with these words, **'For all generations you are to**

declare it a day of festival, for ever.' Ever since the Jewish people
have come together to celebrate the night God rescued their
ancestors from slavery in Egypt. At the heart of the celebration is
the 'Seder Meal' where each ingredient serves as a reminder to the
participants as to what their ancestors had to endure in captivity. The
youngest child present also asks the question, 'Why does this night
differ from all other nights?' Highlighting the central importance of
the celebration. Eventually the father takes a book called the
'Haggadah' and reads the narrative of the Exodus, which includes a
description of the escape from captivity in Egypt. Indeed Moses,
himself exhorted the people never to forget what the Lord had done
by setting them free from slavery. (Exodus 12:24-26) It is important
to remember that what is repeated at the Passover and Seder
celebration is an actual entering into the story of enslavement, flight,
liberation and redemption by God for his people. It is not, however,
a simple remembrance or memorial service but an actual entering
into or participation and therefore sharing in God's life and will for
his people, which is nothing less than total freedom. In other words
it is as if the actual event, that is to say the Exodus, is taking place
again and is therefore in a very real sense, present. This allows all
those who are there to remember but also share directly in the life
saving actions of God. If we are to grasp the fundamental
importance of the Passover for the Jewish people it is vital that we
comprehend this central belief. Indeed, it becomes all the more
important when we recall that Jesus himself would have celebrated
this momentous event in the Jewish religious calendar every single

year of his life right down to the Last Supper.

The next thing for us to grasp is the meaning of some of the prayers said at the Passover, which include petitions for all those people all over the world who are struggling to be free. There are, as we know, many of our fellow human beings who do not enjoy the freedom we have and often take for granted. Slavery, injustice, political corruption and oppression are all too common occurrences, even in our so-called modern world; in such places and under such unjust regimes people long for liberation and freedom. At the Passover Meal such people are remembered and prayed for because, as we know, the Jews were urged never to forget their own experiences of bondage. Below are some references from the Hebrew scriptures which serve to make the important point that because of their own experiences and what God had done for them the Jews were never to forget their obligation to help all those who struggle to be free,

'Defend the weak and the fatherless; uphold the cause of the poor and oppressed.' (Psalm 82:3)

'Is it not to share your food with the hungry and to provide the poor wanderer with shelter – when you see the naked, to clothe them, and not to turn away from your own flesh and blood?' (Isaiah 58:7)

'But you, God, see the trouble of the afflicted; you consider their grief and take it in hand. The victims commit themselves to you; you are the helper of the fatherless.' (Psalm 10:14)

'Remember that you were once salves in Egypt and that God your God redeemed you.' (Deuteronomy 15:15)

The fundamental point to come out of this, however, is vitally important to our understanding of exactly what was going on at the Last Supper. You see the Jew understands that it is God's will for all people to be free because this is what God desires for everyone. Anything, which goes against this, therefore, is contrary to the will of God. So although Jews will pray for this at the Passover meal, prayer alone is not sufficient unless it is translated into action. In other words it is the duty and therefore obligation of every Jew to do whatever he or she can to aid all people to be free. That is to say, to be an active participant in the struggle for liberation for all those who find themselves oppressed or victims of injustice because this is nothing less than the will of God. If then, it is God's will for all people to be free then wherever, or whenever a Jew actively engages in the process of liberation for their fellow human beings it is a direct participation or a sharing in the life of God himself. This is a remarkable claim to make but is central to an understanding of what the Exodus and Passover actually mean. That God heard the cries of his oppressed people, that he intervened in time and space to rescue, deliver and redeem them from slavery in Egypt and that he invites them to share in his life now by engaging actively in the struggle to liberate all oppressed people. This is what it means to experience God in the world today, to reach out to others, the oppressed, the marginalised, the poor, the weak, the downtrodden, the persecuted and all those victims of injustice and not to forget that you were once like them. But equally, to go on from this recognition and offer them the open hand of support, '**Do not harden your heart or close your hand against that poor brother of yours, but be open handed with him and lend him enough for his needs,**' (Deuteronomy 15:8) for in such actions are to be found nothing less than a sharing in the life of God.

This is where, ultimately, the importance of experience is to be found,

- The experience of the Jewish people as slaves in Egypt, something they are told never to forget.
- The experience of the Jewish people at the Exodus as God freed, rescued and delivered them, something they are told to always commemorate and celebrate.
- The experience of the Jewish people today as they share in the life of God through actions which seek liberation for all, something they are told is nothing less than the will of God.

Holy Communion (1 Corinthians 11: 23-26)

In his first letter to the Corinthians Paul describes what he has received about the Last Supper in these words,

'**This is what I received from the Lord, and in turn pass on to you: that on the same night that he was betrayed, the Lord Jesus took some bread, and thanked God for it and broke it, and he** said, 'This is my body, which is for you; do this as a memorial of me.' In the same way he took the cup after supper and said, 'This cup is the new covenant in my blood. Whenever you drink it, do this as a memorial of me.' Until the Lord comes, therefore, every time you eat this bread and drink this cup, you are proclaiming his death.' (1 Corinthians 11:23-26)

This is the only version of the Last Supper read on Maundy Thursday and it surprises some people that one of the more longer versions found in the first three Gospels is not used instead. We shall explain the reason for this a little later but for now it may be helpful to know that this version given to us by Paul is actually older than any found in the Gospels. What it does do though is take us right back to the ancient tradition and practice of the early church by highlighting the most important belief that those initial followers of Jesus had about following his instructions when it came to Holy Communion. It is important to remember, however, that the Last Supper actually took place within the context of the Passover meal, which we have already explored.

One of the most important things for us to note at this stage is the use by Paul here of the word, 'memorial,' sometimes translated as 'remembrance.' The New Testament was originally written in Greek and the word used there to describe this event is 'anamnesis,' (ἀνάμνησις) which effectively cannot be translated into any single English word. This is because it means to make present a past event as if that event were taking place in the here and now. The closet

English word we might have to this is 'memorial' or 'remembrance' but neither does justice to the actual meaning of the word 'anamnesis' itself. This becomes vital to our understanding of what is actually going on when we celebrate Holy Communion. Think back for a moment to our earlier exploration as to how the Jews celebrate Passover, not just as an historical event from the past but as if that event were taking place again but in the present. This is exactly the same principle, which applies to Holy Communion that the events of the Last Supper are actually made physically present during the celebration itself. In other words it is not just a remembering of what Jesus said and did but a making present of them. So when Jesus says, **'This is my body,'** it is his body, which is made present and when He says, **'This cup is the new covenant in my blood,'** then in the same way his very blood is made present. We take Paul's word 'memorial' and infuse it with its authentic and original Greek meaning, to make present a past event. In this way the paschal mystery of Jesus's death and resurrection, the events which took place in that upper room at the Last Supper, his death on the cross and his bodily resurrection to new life all become one in the moment they are celebrated. This, in essence, is the meaning of Holy Communion and on Maundy Thursday it has special significance because Christians are invited to reflect on the mystery of its origins and importance. It is through the celebration of Holy Communion, therefore, that Christians become one with God, sharing directly in his life. What this comes down to then is God's desire for humanity to experience in a direct way his very being. To participate in Holy Communion, therefore, is nothing less than to share in the life of God. All too soon the body of Jesus will literally be broken on the cross and his blood poured out before he eventually dies but after this comes the resurrection and new life. In that upper room all those centuries ago Jesus knowing what would happen to him shares this life with his disciples and in so doing invites all those who would come after to do the same. Every celebration of Holy Communion then is a direct participation in the Lord's life, death and resurrection as he shares his life with his people. This is why Holy Communion is so important and precious to Christians but it should never be separated from what God desires for his people to experience,

- *The experience of the love of God for everyone in the life, death and resurrection of his Son.*
- *The experience of oneness and unity with God, which comes from the most precious body and blood of his Son.*
- *The experience of eternity, as both past and present are made one, in and through, the sacrifice of his Son.*

Loving Service (John 13:1-15)

As I mentioned earlier many people are surprised to learn that a longer version of the Last Supper is not read on Maundy Thursday. The Gospel reading actually comes from John who does not mention the Last Supper at all with reference to bread and wine. Instead, however, what we appear to have is an insight into what the Last

Supper and therefore Holy Communion actually means at a deeper level than described in the first three Gospels. What follows is both shocking and remarkable in how the very essence of God is revealed in the actions of Jesus. John introduces the scene like this, **'he got up from the table, removed his outer garment and, taking a towel, wrapped it around his waist; he then poured water into a basin and began to wash the disciples' feet and to wipe them with the towel he was wearing.'** (John 13: 4-6)

At this point it is worth pausing to reflect on what was actually taking place. To put things in context, within the ancient world, slavery was commonplace. However, even within the slave based system itself there was a hierarchy of importance with the lowest place being occupied by the bond slave. Such slaves were even looked down upon by their fellow slaves because they were given the most demeaning of tasks one of which was foot washing. The bond slave whose role it was to wash feet after a long and dusty journey would often meet invited guests at the door. Such an action was considered to be a great honour and show deep respect for the newly arrived. However, there was no honour or respect in it at all for the bond slave, in fact the reverse was true. You see slaves in the ancient world were seen as nothing more than chattels to be used and abused as their masters saw fit. In this process the slave had no will of their own, no rights, living only to serve their masters.

So what Jesus does at the Last Supper would have been incomprehensible and shocking within the context of the ancient world. For he willingly assumes the condition not just of a slave but also of a common bond slave and washes the feet of his disciples as an act of both service and love. It is not surprising, therefore, that when he approaches Peter he is so surprised, shocked and outraged that he exclaims, **'Never! You shall never wash my feet.'** Jesus then goes on to explain, **'If I do not wash you, you can have nothing in common with me.'** It is quite clear at this point that Peter does not really understand what Jesus is dong and more importantly what it means, when he goes on to say, **'Then Lord, not only my feet, but my hands and my head as well.'** At this point I get the impression that Jesus is, perhaps, a little amused at Peter's lack of understanding when he goes on to say, **'No one who has taken a bath needs washing, he is clean all over.'** So Jesus continues to wash all of the disciple's feet before putting his clothes back on and returning to the table. It is at this point that he engages with his disciples about explaining the meaning of what he has just done to them. **'Do you understand what I have done to you?'** he asks. **'You call me Master and Lord, and rightly so I am. If I, then, the Lord and Master, have washed your feet, you should wash each other's feet. I have given you an example so that you may copy what I have done to you.'** (John 13: 13-15)

This whole passage is stunning in what it reveals about God and discipleship but equally it explains unambiguously the very heart of what Holy Communion really means. We have already seen and explored how through Holy Communion Christians participate directly in the life of God. Jesus makes it abundantly clear that his body would be broken for all people and his blood poured out as an act of supreme and unconditional love. When he washed the feet of his disciples he wanted them and all those who would follow him to know and understand what that meant. What he reveals then, in these actions, is that there is nothing, nothing at all that God is not willing to do for the love of his people and that those who would come after him are invited to do the same. All too soon his body would be literally broken on the cross as an act of pure love but in that upper room Jesus wanted to make it abundantly clear that the invitation to follow him is a call to a life of selfless service and love for others. Very often on Maundy Thursday as well as reflecting on the importance of Holy Communion many Christians are also invited to think about the role of the priesthood in the life of the church. For this reason many priests, imitating the actions of Jesus at the Last Supper, will wash the feet of twelve members of their congregation. It is there on their knees performing this lowly task, in imitation of their Lord and Master that the role of the priest is really to be understood as one of service and love of God's people.

This now brings us back to our central theme that of sharing in the life of God. Jesus invites all those who would follow him to serve and love others in the same way that he did. This is the meaning of what Jesus did at the Last Supper by washing the feet of his disciples. When it comes to us Jesus is saying, 'There is nothing I am not prepared to do for you because I love you and I always will,' but equally he would go on to say, 'now go and do the same for each other.' Here then, at last, everything becomes clear because putting it quite simply, to love and serve others is nothing less than sharing in the life of God. Every time we put other people's needs before our own, we share in the life of God. Every time we get down on our knees and wash each other's feet, we share in the life of God. Every act of kindness, mercy, compassion, forgiveness and love is to share in the life of God. To include the excluded, to go out in search of the lost and the lonely, the rejected, despised, unwanted and unloved and to assure them that they are of value is, once again, to share in the life of God. Every experience that we have of selfless and unconditional love is to share in the life of God as revealed by his Son Jesus Christ on his knees washing the feet of his disciples in that upper room at the Last Supper. This is what John not only wants us to understand but more importantly to go out and live.

Summary

In this chapter we have explored three passages from scripture through the window of Maundy Thursday. This in turn has led us to identify three areas, each of which has enabled us to understand how God desires that we share directly in his life,

- *The Passover – Exodus 12: 1-8, 11-14*
- *Holy Communion – 1 Corinthians 11: 23-26*
- *Loving Service – John 13: 1-15*

The proposal is that these three aspects of our faith bound together in and through the readings express God's desire for humanity to experience and therefore share in his life. For Every time we seek liberation and justice for victims of oppression is to share in the life of God. Every time we participate in Holy Communion, knowing and believing that just like Jesus our bodies must also be broken and poured out for each other, is to share in the life of God. Finally, every time we serve and love one another by getting down on our knees and doing whatever it takes to help those in need, is nothing less than a sharing in the life of God.

CHAPTER SEVEN

Good Friday

The Passion of God

John 18: 1-19:42

When it comes to the crucifixion of Jesus perhaps first and foremost we need to remind ourselves of the facts:

1. He died a violent, cruel and humiliating death.

2. He suffered the death of a common criminal, most of whom were slaves.

3. His own people, including his disciples, abandoned him.

4. He died outside the walls of Jerusalem, symbolising his rejection by the religious establishment.

5. He was mocked and jeered by both the religious leaders and others who stood by and watched.

6. He was executed because he was identified as a threat to the religious and political authorities of the day.

7. He identified himself with all those who were rejected, despised, unwanted and unloved.

8. He cried out to his Father, asking why he had been abandoned.

9. He, for the most part, remained silent.

10. He willingly surrendered his life to his Father.

These facts by themselves are shocking but for the Christian they form the central focus of the Good Friday Liturgy. No other major world religion bases its core belief on the cruel execution of its founder. No other major world religion has, as its main symbol, an image of suffering and death; namely the cross or crucifix.

The first point I want to make concerns the silence of Good Friday. As Jesus is mocked and jeered at by those who watch his cruel and humiliating execution he, for the most part, remains silent; he says nothing. Instead his response is compassion and love. Once again when Jesus cries out, **'My God, my God, why have you forsaken me?'** (Mathew 27:46) his Father remains silent. In this silence what do we see and experience?

- *Powerlessness*
- *Humiliation*
- *Suffering*
- *Cruelty*
- *Pain*
- *Darkness*

- *Death*

The question for us now becomes, 'do we want Jesus to come down from that cross?' The resounding answer to this has to be, '**NO!**' You see we all know, that we suffer too and we do not want to suffer alone. That figure on the cross with all its pain and misery reminds us that when we suffer we never, in fact, suffer alone, he is always with us and the cross tells us that. Indeed when the darkness, pain, misery and cruelty of suffering threaten to overwhelm us he, Jesus, is the only one we can cling to. Without him we would be lost and completely alone.

There are though, perhaps, for all of us times in our own lives when we have felt totally and utterly alone in our suffering with feelings of complete abandonment. Here Jesus speaks to us again from the cross saying, 'I know how you feel.' In his life and ministry Jesus placed all his hope and all his trust in his heavenly Father, then we hear those words uttered by him from the cross which, in turn, echoes through our own lives and experiences, '**My God, my God, why have you forsaken me?**' (Mathew 27:46). At this point our own hearts threaten to break, 'how could this be happening?' we might ask. We might even be tempted to conclude that the Father had actually abandoned the Son and if he had abandoned him then what about us? What happens at this point is crucial to our understanding of what is going on through the crucifixion of Jesus and why Good Friday is so important. You see the truth is that the Father never, ever, abandoned the Son. Instead the Father experienced the pain, suffering and humiliation of the Son at the same time too. This is why it is perfectly correct to refer to Good Friday as nothing less than the **'Passion of God.'**

The effect of this is to completely transform our understanding of God. This is because on the one hand Jesus, the Son, through his agony on the cross brings suffering humanity to the Father, whilst at the same time bringing the Father to suffering humanity. As a result perfect communion is achieved, that is to say, at oneness, between God and humanity through the pain and suffering of his Son, Jesus. That is why it is perfectly correct to say that all suffering is a participation in the suffering of God. This is why all of our hope and all of our trust is placed in Jesus on that cross. It is important to note, however, that we are never told the 'why?' of suffering. Only that God suffers with us and that suffering is not the end because the cross eventually leads to the resurrection and eternal life with him. From this point of view we can conclude, however, that the crucifixion of Jesus is the most decisive event in human history through which God saves the human race. Equally it also allows us, along with the resurrection, as we shall see, to share in the very life of God himself.

We now need to turn our attention to the question we have just alluded to, 'from what does God save the human race?' At this stage I would identify three areas, all of which I would classify as being enemies of both God and humanity, to focus our attention on:

- Sin
- Satan/evil
- Death

Once again the next point to be made is crucial if we are to understand what is going on in and through the crucifixion of Jesus. There is, in fact, no change on the cross from what Jesus taught, lived and preached throughout his entire earthly ministry and that is only love can redeem and save the human race from the three enemies identified above. Only love makes us who and what we are as made in the image of God and therefore truly human. What the cross teaches us therefore is a new language and a new way of being, which is love. Christ loves to the end. When faced with the pain, misery, suffering, cruelty, abandonment, humiliation, mockery and death of the cross, God's answer was love. Without such love nothing, in fact, makes any kind of sense. It is in and through the **Crucified God** that meaning is given to everything but only through the love it reveals. This I would now suggest is the supreme truth that God reveals to the human race from the cross and this is exactly why Jesus came to set us free from Satan, Sin and Death because in the words of Christ himself, **'the truth will set you free.'** (John 832) It is this truth, which reveals the nature and the very being of God and it is this truth, which makes us truly human. The hope for humanity then is to be found on that cross where the love of God in and through his Son is made present for all to see.

So what happens now? What should our response be to the

revelation of such overwhelming love and how are we to interpret it and apply it in our own lives today? As we gaze upon the image of the **Crucified God** what issues forth is nothing less than an invitation from Jesus himself to follow him but to do this he makes it clear that, **'Anyone who wishes to follow me must deny himself, take up his cross and follow me.'** (Mathew 16:24) This now becomes the key to understanding both our humanity and what it means to be a disciple of Jesus. Here we find an invitation to be part of transformed existence or a completely new way of both living and loving. To do this, however, the Christian must stand in direct opposition to everything responsible for crucifying Jesus, that is to say,

- *Injustice*
- *Oppression*
- *Persecution*
- *Cruelty*
- *Lies*
- *Abuse*
- *Intolerance*
- *Mockery*
- *Hate*

Equally like Jesus, the Christian must also oppose such evil and sin with the weapons of,

- **Mercy**

- **Compassion**
- **Forgiveness**
- **Truth**
- **Justice**
- **Love**

Jesus makes it abundantly clear that to follow such a path will inevitably lead to our own suffering but if the Christian is to make the world more human, then just like for him, the price to be paid may well be a high one. In his book **'The Cost of Discipleship,'** (1) Dietrich Bonhoeffer consistently makes the point that there will always be a cost to discipleship in following Jesus. Indeed he also pushes the point home even further by saying that without cost there can be no true discipleship. Bonhoeffer himself, a Christian minister, living in Germany during the Second World War who opposed both the Nazis party and Adolf Hitler was to pay the ultimate price for such opposition when he was executed. If then we are to be part of Christ's mission to make the world in which we live a better place, more just and more human for everyone, there will be a price to pay. However, if we are to do this we need to look upon the crucified Christ in all that pain, misery and suffering and recognise something quite remarkable, ourselves! This is in and of itself supremely challenging but it goes right to the very heart of the Good Friday revelation, that God in Christ invites us to be part of his redeeming mission. This is God's challenge to us, to join him, to be one with him, to be part of his community the church, charged with making his creation better for all people but especially those living on the margins. At this point we might be tempted to say, 'this is just too much,' but listen again to the words of Jesus, '**Take my yoke upon you and learn from me, for I am meek and humble of heart, and you will find rest for your souls. For my yoke is easy and my burden light.**' (Matthew 11:29-30) It is true that God gives us a task if we accept his invitation but we cannot nor should we complete this task alone, instead we need to see and believe that he is always with us helping us shoulder the burden, for '**I am with you always, to the end of the world.**' (Matthew 28:20)

Yet to share in his mission is also, as he makes abundantly clear, to share in his fate,

'**You will be hated by all because of my name.**' (Matthew 10:22)

'**If they persecuted me, they will persecute you.**' (John 15:20)

'**If the world hates you, be aware that it hated me before it hated you.**' (John 15:18)

'**Blessed are you when people insult you and persecute you and utter all kinds of calumnies against you for my sake.**' (Matthew 5:11)

If Jesus then stood with the powerless and the voiceless, those who had been stripped of every human dignity and was opposed by those who had most to lose, that is to say the powerful, we can see clearly just how the fate of Jesus was ultimately sealed. As he neared

Jerusalem Caiaphas the High Priest, the Pharisees and the Sadducees all of whom had protected status under Roman rule with a guaranteed income and life-style had the most to lose if the people followed Jesus. Knowing that their whole way of life was under threat they plotted to remove the problem, that is to say Jesus by colluding with the occupying power, Rome. Earlier we said that in the crucifixion Jesus was confronted with three things all of which stood in direct opposition to God, Sin, Satan/Evil and death. Now he would be confronted with how these forces took human form in,

Religion through Caiaphas, the Pharisees and the Sadducees

Politics through Pontius Pilate

Power through Rome

All of which was to serve self-interest.

The response of Jesus and therefore God to all of these forces was to **Love**. From the beginning of his life right through to the end Jesus confronted the world and therefore humanity with the love of God. It was a love the world did not understand, Saint Paul put it like this, **'none of the rulers of this age comprehended it. If they had, they would not have crucified the Lord of glory.'** (I Corinthians 2:8) In Christ on the cross on Good Friday then we see what the love of God actually looks like but what extends from that cross is also an invitation to the human race to love like him and in so doing to become more human, more of what God calls us to be. The truth is then that when we suffer, we never suffer alone because in and through Christ we are at one with him and through him to the Father. Our mission and, therefore the mission of the church is to incarnate, make flesh, in our own lives this central truth of our faith, which is to love just like him. A crucified love, lived right through to the end despite the terrible cost but which led ultimately to resurrection.

This is why the crucifix is so central to Catholics as a symbol of faith in Christ. It stands at the very heart of every Catholic Church, every Catholic School and every Catholic home. It is worn around the neck of many Catholic Christians lying close to their heart. It is something that we should never take for granted because it is a constant reminder of what the love of God actually looks like, crucified love, revealed by a **Crucified God** so that all should know, believe and understand that there is literally nothing that he is not prepared to go through because of his love for us.

'For God so loved the world that he gave his only Son, so that everyone who believes in him may not perish but may attain eternal life.' (John 3:16)

The final thing then for us to keep constantly in mind is what our communion with God in Christ actually means when it comes to Good Friday. In fact it is nothing less than a crucified life, in whatever form it may take and it will be different for each and every single one of us but lived through to the end it will always lead to resurrection.

(1.) 'The Cost of Discipleship,' by Dietrich Bonhoeffer, SCM Press 2015

GOOD FRIDAY

A REFLECTION ON THE LOVE OF GOD AS REVEALED IN THE PASSION OF CHRIST

The cross becomes the new language of God's love

Good Friday sees the beginning of **new language**; it comes from the cross and is revealed in and through Christ's sacrifice. It is God's own **language** and comes into existence at great cost. If we are going to learn how to understand this **new language** and apply it in our own lives then we need to listen very carefully to the words of Jesus so that we too can live the **language of love.**

Seven words from the cross – the new language of God's love

1. **'Father forgive them for they don't know what they are doing'**

Forgiveness is seen in the language of **love**, self-emptying, self-sacrificial **love**. By surrendering everything to the Father Jesus surrenders everything to us. Such is the new **language of love.**

2. **'Today you will be with me in paradise'**

The promise of heaven; only to a convicted, condemned and dying criminal. Salvation is offered to the most wretched, the most improbable, and the least likely. Such is the new **language of love.** Salvation is offered to you and me!

3. 'Woman behold your son. Son behold your mother'

So speaks the **language of love.** For it is the language of an intimate embrace. If only we could realise that we are wrapped and enfolded in the loving arms of Christ himself.

4. 'My God my God why have your forsaken me?'

Silence! For a while the **language of love** can only be found in the silence of the Father and yet **love** remains.

5. 'I am thirsty'

God thirsts for our **love**, even as we thirst for his. Yet only the love of God as revealed in Christ Jesus our Lord can ever quench our deepest thirst.

6. 'It is finished'

Can a broken life heal the world? Can **love** defeat hate? Can hope overcome despair? Can life triumph over death? Such is the **language of crucified love.**

7. 'Into your hands I commend my spirit'

Christ lets go of his life and trusts in the Father's **love.** We are invited to let go of our lives and trust in Christ's **love** for us. Such is the **language of love.**

For now the sky darkens and our crucified world longs for the light of Easter.

Christ now whispers – 'trust in me and I promise you all will be well.'

This is the **language of love**

Crucified.

But soon to be risen!

CHAPTER EIGHT

The Easter Vigil

'Why look among the dead for someone who is alive?'

Luke 24: 1-12

Introduction

For Catholics the Easter Vigil is the high point of the liturgical year. Indeed, it is so important that before I proceed to explore its meaning and significance through the Gospel of Luke, I felt compelled to write a preparatory introduction. We have just examined the **Passion of God** and one of the things we need to keep at the forefront of our minds is the cost and therefore the price God, himself, paid to set the human race free from Sin, Satan and Death. It is, if truth were told, one of those things that, perhaps, we all at times take for granted but this is something we must constantly guard against. In the film **'The Passion of the Christ'** (2004) directed by Mel Gibson, critics made the claim that it was just too graphic in its portrayal of the crucifixion. Yet, the process of crucifixion itself was brutal and barbaric, there is no way to escape this basic truth and we should never attempt to reduce it to anything less. However, nor should we ever seek to exalt suffering for its own sake but the simple truth is that God's Son died an horrific death on a cross constructed to maximise pain, humiliation and suffering. Nor should we ever forget that this was done to God by his own creation. As we move from death to life then we must concede that this just did not happen, it was part of a process, part of a lifesaving event, in and through which God was the chief participant. The celebration of **'The Sacred Paschal Triduum'** is as we have already alluded to something, which God also invites us to experience and therefore participate in, now. This is because the lifesaving actions of God cannot be separated from those whom he loves, that is to say humanity. Therefore God invites his people to journey with him from death to life as both Sin and Satan are vanquished. This is why the Easter Vigil is so important in the life of the Church, it is the night above all nights, it is the night like no other and it is the night on which everything changed and would never be the same again.

Having considered the importance of the Easter Vigil we now need to move onto something else, which is also essential if we are to understand and comprehend its true significance. As we enter the Easter Vigil we must be prepared to change if these lifesaving events are ever going to impact on our lives. So, no matter where we are in our journey of faith we must be open to change or transformation but from the inside out. This is something that we must take seriously and it needs to be given due time and consideration in our lives. In this sense preparation and instruction is very important. In the early days of the church up to a year would be spent preparing candidates for baptism at the Easter Vigil and this is something which has been recaptured in recent times through the Roman

Catholic Initiation of Adults (RCIA) programme. Yet preparation is needed for all of us if we are truly to understand the momentous life changing actions of God as celebrated through the Easter Vigil. Therefore I would go so far as to say that if we are not prepared to change or to be transformed by the Easter Vigil then we should stay away and at the same time keep well clear of the Gospel. This is because both of them by the grace of God are meant to literally change our lives forever! In summary this how Saint Paul put it,

'We are afflicted on all sides but not crushed, bewildered but not sunk in despair, persecuted but not abandoned, struck down but not destroyed. We always carry around in our body the death of Jesus, so that the life of Jesus may also be manifested in our body. For in our lives we are constantly being given up to death for Jesus's sake, so that the life of Jesus may be revealed in our mortal flesh. (2 Corinthians 4: 8-12)

All of us should demand, therefore, appropriate preparation for the Easter Vigil with every fibre of our being. It is not something that we should just drift into or see as just another church service, instead it should excite us to the point that we tremble in anticipation of what we are about to share in, which is nothing less than the lifesaving actions of God himself for humanity.

The Gospel of life (Luke 24: 1-12)

As we come to this wonderful Gospel reading, which lies at the heart of the Easter Vigil we need to pause a little and take the time to reflect on what was going on in the hearts and minds of the followers of Jesus at the time. The first point to make is that faith in the risen Lord did not just happen nor was it something that they could work out for themselves. Instead what we find in their hearts and minds was total and utter confusion. This in turn led to doubts and uncertainties. After all, the tomb was empty, they had seen and possibly touched the burial cloth of Jesus, he was dead, and they knew that as a fact but what had happened to the body? What was going on? You see for those early followers of Jesus resurrection was something that he talked to them about but they struggled to believe and therefore comprehend what it all meant, after all things like that just do not happen! Take for example Mary Magdalene, John tells us, in his Gospel, that early on that first Easter morning she went looking for the body of Jesus and found the tomb empty. She did not immediately conclude that he had risen and in so doing had conquered Satan, Sin and Death. Nor did she conclude that everything had changed and would never be the same again, that there had been a new creation and that God through his Son had transformed life itself. For Mary Magdalene, the tomb was empty the body of Jesus was gone and she was confused not transformed. Her experience, therefore, though totally understandable was reduced to missing Jesus without whom her life now had no meaning or purpose. (John 20: 11-15)

Now let us look more closely at what Luke has to say. A group of women, motivated by their love for Jesus, head to the tomb to anoint his body **'with the spices they had prepared.'** They are finding it impossible to forget their Lord and Master and want to be close to him again even though he is dead. Perhaps they are talking about him as they approach the tomb, after all he had treated them like no other man had done before with such dignity, respect and love. On the other hand they may have been weeping as they recalled his cruel and brutal death. However, **'on entering, the tomb, they discovered that the body of Jesus was not there.'** Or in other words they did not find what they expected and this led to confusion and doubt, **'as they stood there not knowing what to think.'** Then two men appeared **'in brilliant white clothes'** and the women were terrified but the men said to them, **'Why look among the dead for someone who is alive? He is not here; he has risen.'** (Luke 24: 1-6)

At this point I am going to hit the pause button and ask a difficult question of both myself and of you the reader. Where does our faith in the resurrection of Jesus come from? I know that I have spoken many times to many different people, in a variety of contexts, right across the age range from small children right up to adults about the resurrection of Jesus and it has not led them to faith. What have I learned from this? That faith and therefore belief in the resurrection of Jesus from the dead does not come about simply because we have learned about it from teachers, catechists or dare I say even from the clergy! So where does it come from then? First and foremost we must be open to belief in the resurrection and to do this we have to make our own journey of faith. Now we can go back to what those two men said to the women in the empty tomb and this is vitally important, **'Why look among the dead for someone who is alive?'** If then we are to search for and indeed find Jesus, then it must be among the living, this is because Jesus is alive and not dead! Of course we must be open to Jesus and seek him with all our heart, with all our soul, with our entire mind and with our very being but he is alive and we must never forget that. If then we are to find Jesus and faith in his resurrection from the dead we must listen to the voice of those men on that first Easter morning who in the dark and empty tomb told those women and in turn us, **'Why look among the dead for someone who is alive?' He is not here; he has risen.'** (Luke 24:5)

At this point I want us to stop again and take some time to pause and reflect and for us to be honest with ourselves when it comes to questions of faith and practice. In the Gospel of Mark Jesus says this, **'He is not the God of the dead but of the living?'** (Mark 12:27). He makes the same point earlier in Luke too, **'He is not the God of the dead, but of the living, for in his sight all are alive.'** (Luke 20:38) Sounds familiar? That is because we have already heard the same thing in our Easter Vigil Gospel. So how would you describe your faith and your belief in the resurrection? Let us face it most of us become overfamiliar, comfortable with our faith over the years and it becomes less exciting, less life-giving even less challenging but does it really have to be this way? The answer is, of course not but what do we do? We need to go back to the tomb and those words of the two men to the women, **'Why look among the dead for someone who is alive?'**

What follows next requires us to be both honest and brave. It is also requires us to be changed, to be transformed by God's grace. We need to follow the instructions of those two men to the women in that empty tomb and search for the risen and life giving Son of God among the living. Remember that in and through the resurrection everything changed and nothing would ever be the same again, **'I have come that you may have life and have it in abundance.'** (John 10:10) So we must look for Jesus where his Spirit is giving life, we must find him where his Spirit lives, we must discover him where in and through his Spirit faith is received as a gift and where that same faith is lived out in lives of love and service to others. For the Spirit of the resurrected Lord, his life giving and ever creative Spirit is to be found in communities where he is recognised as the one who gives them life and who upholds and sustains them in being. Call to mind again his words, **'For where two or three are gathered together in my name, I am there in their midst.'** (Matthew 18:20) This is the Spirit of Jesus who reaches out and touches our hearts and who invites us, with him, to build a better world. This is the Spirit of Jesus who through his resurrection creates all things new, including you and me, **'consequently, anyone united to Christ is a new creation,'** (2 Corinthians 17) and so invites us to be transformed by his grace. This is the Spirit of

Jesus, which charges us to go, just like him, in search of the lost and the lonely, the despised and the rejected, the forgotten and the wretched, the voiceless, the weak, the oppressed and the unloved and to assure them of his love. Where Jesus is at the centre of such communities and such lives he will touch our hearts, our lives and our very souls, then others will know because they will see that he is not dead he is alive because he lives in us.

If we can see this and more importantly believe it everything would change and nothing would ever be the same again. It is this, which is the **Good News** (Gospel) and it is this, which should excite, enthuse and humble us all at one and the same time as we experience the power of his resurrection to change our lives. This is what flows out of the Easter vigil and it is both challenging and dangerous at the same time. If we want our lives to be transformed by the grace of his resurrection then after suitable preparation we should, with all humility, go to the Easter Vigil but be warned we will not leave the same person we came in as!

What changes is our relationship with Christ, our relationship with others and indeed even our relationship with ourselves as we become bound to his mission to transform the world. We cannot, however, live our lives on a perpetual high. Look for example at what happened when the women returned from the tomb to tell the disciples what they had experienced, **'but this story of theirs seemed pure nonsense, and they did not believe them.'** Still when this happens and it will to all of us, do not fall into despair because

Christ invites not to stay in the darkness of the tomb but to come out and live. The Gospel, in fact, ends on a high,

'Peter, however, went running to the tomb. He bent down and saw the binding cloths, but nothing else; he then went back home, amazed at what had happened.' (Luke 24:12)

To go to the Easter Vigil with humility but with a heightened sense of expectation, to enter the darkness of the tomb with Christ and to experience our own spiritual rebirth is to be literally transformed by his grace. In the same way, therefore, we too should also leave, **'amazed at what has happened.'** Yet the story does not end there and nor should it, indeed just like the resurrection, it is for us too, a new beginning because what we have celebrated and experienced should change how we live. Grace has come to us through the most costly of sacrifices, our calling re-energised by the resurrection of Christ, is to live our lives in a new way with him in our midst, the **God of the living and not of the dead.**

CHAPTER NINE

Easter Day

The Empty Tomb

'The Light shines in the darkness and the darkness cannot overcome it' (John 1:5)

John 20: 1-9

In his book **'The God of Surprises,'** (1) the late Gerard Hughes SJ makes the point that we cannot control God. Yet, at times, it is true that all of us fall into the trap of expecting God to behave in the way we think he should behave and therefore do what we want him to do. Sadly what this results in is our failure to let God be God and this is exactly the point that Gerard Hughes is making. The prophet Isaiah puts it like this, **'For my thoughts are not your thoughts, neither are your ways my ways, says the Lord.'** (Isaiah 55:8) If we are not careful, therefore, what we are left with is a preconditioned way of believing in God outside of which we cannot and will not allow him to act. Where then is **'The God of Surprises'** the God who acts according to his will and not ours? Ask yourself this question then as we celebrate the greatest feast in the Christian calendar, when was the last time your heart burned within you?

When was the last time you felt touched by God's grace to the point you experienced, literally, the embrace of his gentle, all-consuming love? Some people say this is not possible, faith is not like that but is this true and is that what God desires? You see the danger for us is the temptation to limit God to what we have become used to, familiar with, comfortable with, outside of which God, as far as we are concerned does not act. To do this and without realising it we are, in fact, placing limitations on God and completely and at the same time unintentionally impoverishing our own faith and how we can experience it. The key is to allow God to be God and to behave according to his will and not ours for remember the words of the Lord's Prayer, **'Thy will be done on earth as it is in heaven.'** (Matthew 6: 9-13) Easter takes this way of understanding our faith and blows everything apart, bringing love where there was only hate; light where there was only darkness and life where there was only death. But nobody expected it, nobody really believed in it and nobody saw it coming for this was and is **'The God of Surprises'** in action.

Have you ever had a 'eureka moment?' They normally come after weeks, months even years of prolonged activity. Let me give you an example. I have for many years been involved in academic work which has taken up lengthy periods of research, study, prayer, reading, reflection and eventually writing. Yet there have been times when I have, metaphorically, run into a brick wall. I have been trying to understand something or explain a complex issue in a straightforward way but fail to make the break-through. I get stuck, my mind goes blank and I hit a dead end. When this happens my mind ends up wondering all over the place as I try to get that break-through but nothing comes of it no matter how hard I try. The books end up not speaking to me anymore and the complex issues just become too difficult to break down. The temptation at this point, to be honest, is to give up. So what do I do? For a while I do stop looking, I let go and switch off and I end up not forcing the issue anymore. When the break-through actually does come it appears to be completely at random. I might be watching a programme on television, listening to the radio, having a chance conversation with someone, reading a magazine or a newspaper or even just day dreaming but all of a sudden the penny drops, I see the way through the maze and everything falls into place. This is the 'eureka moment,' something which appears to be completely random but which sets in motion a process which helps makes sense of a complex and perplexing set of facts which my brain found to be completely inaccessible. Hence, my reasoning or my thinking process by itself was not enough but when the trigger happened it helped me make sense out of everything. At this point remember Sir Isaac Newton? Gravity all of sudden made sense for him when, of all things, an apple fell on his head. This was his 'eureka moment.' I can only define it as a sudden burst of realisation, which gives rise to a cry of exclamation! The key, however, to getting the point I am trying to make is that it involves some kind of catalyst, which all of a sudden sheds light on understanding something that has previously eluded you. Now I know what you are thinking, 'What has this go to do with Easter?' Well the answer is, in fact, everything. All I am asking for, at the moment, is a little patience and your willingness to allow God to be **'The God of Surprises.'**

Now let us turn our attention to the Gospel reading for Easter day, John 20:1-9. We are told, **'It was very early on the first day of the week and still dark, when Mary of Magdala came to the tomb.'** I cannot help but wonder what was going through Mary's mind at the time as she made that journey and what was she expecting to find? After all she saw Jesus die, saw him buried in the tomb, perhaps, even saw the stone rolled across the entrance. So then was death on her mind? Was she going to anoint the body of Jesus as the other Gospel writers tell us? Did she expect to see guards at the tomb? I cannot help but wonder about how she felt. Her heart must have been broken, perhaps she still wept and could not imagine life without her Lord. After all there is no indication at all, in John, that Mary had any thought whatsoever about the resurrection. Why should she? Was it because even for her there was, in fact, no place for **'The God of Surprises,'** the God who acts outside of our expectations? Mary had spent a long time with Jesus and he had talked about his death and resurrection on more than one occasion but had all that been forgotten now, after all people just do not rise from the dead, do they?

But then she saw something that she did not expect to see, **'that the stone had been moved away from the tomb'** and there were no guards. What did she think now, I wonder, that this does not make sense? But no matter what was going through her mind she did not enter the tomb, instead she ran to Peter and John and said, **'They have taken the Lord out of the tomb and we don't know where they have put him.'** Notice that, once again, there is no mention of the resurrection, it was not the first thing that came to Mary's mind, instead she made the assumption that the body of Jesus must simply have been taken.

Now Peter and John rush to the tomb and on reaching it first John hesitates and does not go in. I wonder why? Why does John not run straight into the tomb looking for answers as to where the body of Jesus was? However, he does see the linen cloths lying on the ground. I wonder what he thinks now. What has happened? Where is Jesus? Who took him? I think this moment taken by John is really important as he processes not only what he is seeing but also what it actually means. Peter on the other hand does not hesitate and rushes straight in, he also sees, **'the linen cloths on the ground and also the cloth that had been over his head.'** At this point John finally enters the tomb and we are told that something quite remarkable happens. For a moment, however, let us go back to that period of hesitation by John at the entrance to the tomb and reflect on what might have been going through his mind. Firstly, the stone had been moved and quite clearly it should not have been; this was his second surprise after Mary had told him the body of Jesus was gone. Then secondly he saw the linen cloths on the floor where they should not have been and this was his third surprise. Finally, there was no body, what Mary had told him was true. Did John now begin to put together the fragments of what Jesus had said to him all those years ago, **'Unless a grain of wheat falls into the ground and dies it remains a single grain. But if it dies it produces much fruit.'** (John 12: 24) and **'And when I am lifted up from the earth, I will draw all people to myself.'** (12:33) 'Could it be, no that would not be possible.' With all these thoughts going through his mind John finally enters the tomb and this becomes his 'eureka moment.' He sees the empty stone shelf on which should have laid the dead body of Jesus, he sees, once again, the linen cloths lying on the ground and suddenly they become the catalyst for his proclamation of faith because we are told, **'he saw and he believed.'** It is one of those moments in scripture, which should raise the hairs on the back of our neck. **'The God of Surprises'** blows away all our preconceived ideas about how he should act for this God brings love where there was only hatred, light where there was only darkness and life where there was only death. John, we are told, experiences that break-through directly, all of a sudden his understanding of who God is and what God has done becomes illuminated by what he sees in that empty tomb. I can only imagine John standing there dumb-founded and at the same time elated by this revelation from God. He had spent somewhere between one and three years with Jesus and now all of a sudden everything made perfect sense. As if to confirm this we are told, **'Till this moment they had failed to understand the teaching of scripture, that he must rise form the dead.'** The only question now remaining is, 'what does this mean for us?'

It is vitally important not to confine the resurrection to an event, in history, which took place over 2,000 years ago. God desires that we live and move and have our being in and through him who gives us life, **'I have come that you may have life,'** Jesus tells us. Now of course it is essential for us to believe that Jesus actually rose physically from the dead but equally we also need to believe that he shares that new life with us, now. That we can participate in his risen life now and moreover we can see signs of that risen and therefore new life everywhere. When through faith our eyes are opened something remarkable happens, something, which John in that empty tomb grasped all those centuries ago, that the resurrection must also take place in us too! Very often, though, we need that catalyst which for John was the empty tomb and the linen cloths lying on the ground. Suddenly for him everything, at last, made sense but for this to happen he had spent, as we have already said, somewhere between one and three years with Jesus. Most of us too have spent much of our lives with him and yet he still invites us to open our eyes so that we also may see and experience the resurrection in the here and now. At Easter this also should make the hairs on the back of our necks stand up as the risen Christ bursts from the tomb offering to all the gift of new life. Let us now see how this might happen for all of us in a new and exciting way.

In his book, **'True Resurrection,'** (2) Harry Williams CR makes the important point that the resurrection is something to be lived and experienced now through the eyes of faith. I remember once, for example, going for a walk and as I did so passed a thorn bush. Then in the midst of winter we were hit with a hard ground frost, followed by a period of heavy snow. The land-scape became bleak and harsh, the thorn bush looked dead though its sharp prickles remained and I remember thinking, 'how is it possible anything could ever live under such condition?' Then one day as I passed the same thorn bush, in early spring, it seemed to have sprung into life and right there in the midst of it stood a single beautiful golden daffodil. Life had come out of what had appeared to be only death or putting it another way – resurrection! This is the point made by Harry Williams in his book that the resurrection is something to be lived and experienced – now. Remember what Jesus said, '**I am the resurrection and the life,**' (John 11:25) and that resurrected life came out of the darkness of the tomb. It can, however, come out of our own darkness too. Remember that 'eureka moment' I spoke about earlier, that's resurrection. The elderly person in the care home who never receives a single visitor but one day the local primary school turn up to play games with the residents, that's resurrection. The moment a baby is born and held for the first time by Mum and Dad and their hearts just melt, that's resurrection. To know, believe and understand that you are loved and cherished by another person who wants to spend the rest of their lives with you and you alone, that's resurrection. The child placed with foster or adoptive parents who for the first time in their lives know that they are actually wanted for who they are, that's resurrection. Very often we do not realise it at the time, instead realisation comes later, as it did with John but it is still resurrection.

We now live in difficult, even dark times and the temptation amidst the darkness of the CARONAVIRUS, COVID-19, is for some people to lose hope or even lapse into despair but God in Christ invites us, especially at Easter, to take a different course. Although we are now, metaphorically at least, in the darkness of the tomb, Christ is our light, who shines in our hearts and bids us turn to him, 'open your eyes and look at the world with the eyes of faith and see what happens,' resurrection!

Resurrection in all those doctors and nurses who, literally, everyday are putting their own lives on the line to relieve the pain and suffering of others. I have seen exhausted doctors and nurses, living in caravans close to the hospitals where they work, going back time and time again to help others, that's resurrection. For all those key workers whether they are police officers, paramedics, postal staff, supermarket workers, those who work in care homes, lorry drivers and so on simply just carrying on so that others may live, that's resurrection. Then what about all those people who simply feel the need to say 'thank you' to the **National Health Service** by joining in spontaneous applause, that's resurrection. Then there are all those volunteers, most of whom we will never know anything about but who simply feel compelled to put the needs of others before themselves that too is resurrection.

You see, as I said right at the beginning, God is not confined to anything. God goes where he wants; God does what he wants, for God is '**The God of Surprises.**' As Christians this should fill our hearts with great joy, to see the life of God before our very eyes, risen in the service and love people offer to each other in the darkness of the tomb. This Easter then take the time, with John, to pause at the entrance to that tomb, see the linen cloths lying on the ground, then look up, see and believe that Christ is risen, open your eyes, embrace his resurrected life and step out of the darkness and into the light.

For,

Alleluia, Christ is risen!

He is risen indeed, Alleluia!

1. 'The God of Surprises,' by Gerard Hughes (DLT, 2008)

2. 'True Resurrection,' by Harry Williams (Mitchell Beazley, 1975)

CHAPTER TEN

Easter

The Road to Emmaus in One Word

Luke 24: 13-55

Very often when I am trying to prepare something whether that be a homily, talk, lecture or a lesson I ask myself one fundamental question, 'how can I make this as simple as possible for people to understand?' Jesus, somehow, always managed to do this, whilst at the same time allowing people to access the infinite love of God. So my starting point is often to identify a word, just one word upon which my whole proposal will be hung. When reflecting on the Gospel of Luke and his description of the two disciples of Jesus as they travelled to Emmaus the one word which came to mind for me was **presence** and it is through this word that I want to explore the Easter story again.

First, however, I want to go back to an earlier account in John when Jesus appeared to his disciples after his resurrection from the dead. In John 20: 19-31, we are told that the disciples knew Jesus had risen from the dead because they had already seen him. However, such knowledge and proclamation of the Easter message do not in themselves appear to be enough. Instead the disciples seem to be missing something, which is the experience of Jesus being alive with them. As a result they lock themselves away in a room because, as John tells us, they were afraid. Everything changes, however, when Jesus appears to them and here we have an important insight as to what John is trying to tell us. It is only when Jesus stands at the very heart of our lives and of our community that he, in turn, becomes the true source of our peace and joy. The minute Jesus appears to the disciples John tells us they were, **'filled with joy,'** and here we have it, the **presence** of Jesus changes everything. Christian lives and communities are transformed when it is possible to see the **presence** of Jesus in the midst of them. It is the **presence** of Jesus, which allows us to overcome our fears and to fill our hearts with peace and joy. However, this can only ever happen when we recognise the **presence** of Jesus with us as a reality. The minute we lose this we become lost just like the disciples who locked themselves away in the upper room because they were afraid all those years ago. The key to everything then is Jesus and his **presence** with us here and now, it is this and only this, which will transform our lives as we recognise him in our midst.

Now we can return to Luke and his description of two disciples as they journeyed to Emmaus. In the early days of the church one group of people, quite naturally stood out, those who had actually physically seen the risen Jesus. So Peter, John and Mary Magdalene are just three examples of those who had unique experiences of the resurrection and therefore the **presence** of Jesus. Indeed, it could be said that it is through these unique experiences that each of them had, that they were led to their belief in the resurrected Lord. But what about those who became followers of Jesus later and who, therefore, did not have such experiences? Of course this applies to us too as we also have not experienced the resurrected Lord in the same way those early disciples did. How can we today then experience the **presence** of Jesus in our lives and in our communities so that our faith in him is upheld and sustained? This is exactly the issue being explored by Luke through the two disciples as they travelled to Emmaus.

Let us note, first of all, how down they are as they made their journey, '**Our own hope had been that he would be the one to set Israel free.**' Obviously they are sad and disillusioned and it would seem that they have lost their faith in Jesus. You see for them things had gone horribly wrong, Jesus was dead and even though some women had gone to the tomb and found it empty, '**but of him they saw nothing,**' they had no direct experience of the resurrection of Jesus to sustain them. We all know, I am sure, many people who have drifted away from the Church and, perhaps, there have even been times in our own lives when we have found it difficult to believe. This is when we can walk this walk with the disciples as they made their way to Emmaus. They seem to have lost all hope and they are questioning everything they ever believed about Jesus, 'could it be that they were wrong all along?' 'Was everything just an illusion?' 'What now is the point of anything, anymore?' Many people today feel like that and you, the reader, may also be feeling exactly like that as you read this but let me assure you that such feelings are OK because they are honest and the first person we need to be honest with is ourselves and let us face it God knows exactly how we feel because we can hide nothing from him.

Going back to Luke, it would seem that completely unnoticed to the disciples Jesus has been following them and listening to what they had been saying to each other. Eventually he catches up and joins them. From this point on Jesus walks with them and begins to have a conversation with them. Speaking directly to their despondency he says,

'You foolish men! So slow to believe the full message of the prophets! Was it not ordained that the Christ should suffer and so enter into his glory?' Then, starting with Moses and going through all the prophets, he explained to them the passages throughout the scriptures that were about himself.'

However, despite all of this those two disciples were still not able to recognise who Jesus was, Luke puts it like this, **'something prevented them from recognising him.'** Once again there are many people in the world today who do not recognise who Jesus is and as a result he has no meaning for them. In the same way we may know many members of our own families and friends for whom Jesus is an irrelevance. So here is the question, 'what can those two disciples do to recognise who is **present** with them standing, in fact, right by their side?' Here we need to reflect on the whole incident as described to us by Luke. What is quite remarkable, however, is that throughout the whole passage those same two disciples never stopped talking about Jesus. Right from the beginning we are told, **'they were talking together about all that had happened.'** After Jesus joins them and enquires about their conversation they are more than happy to tell him, **'All about Jesus of Nazareth, who proved to be a great prophet by the things that he said and did in the sight of God and the whole people.'** They then go on to describe how he was put to death and what followed in the discovery of the empty tomb. Jesus then tells them how all of this was part of God's plan for his Christ right from the beginning. In other words the whole passage becomes a reflection on the revelation of God in his Son through the scriptures. Although they did not recognise who Jesus was at the time, later they were able to say, **'Did not our hearts burn within us as he talked to us on the road and explained the scriptures to us?'**

What this highlights for us is the importance of never forgetting Jesus both in our own lives and in the lives of our communities. To do this we need to recognise the **presence** of Jesus in the midst of us, and the first way to do this is through the scriptures. At the same time we need to combine this with prayer and reflection because we need to ask God to guide us, through the grace of his Holy Spirit, to a greater understanding and appreciation of his Son. This means allowing our hearts to be drawn ever deeper into scripture, which is nothing less than God's word speaking to our very souls. There we need to discover the meaning of his message and his actions and the effect they can have on our lives. In and through scripture God invites us to recognise the **presence** of his Son there in the midst of us just waiting to be discovered. We can ask Jesus, in faith, to reach down into the deepest parts of our souls and to touch us in such a way that his words awaken within us a sense of his **presence** so that our very hearts begin to burn.

However, this alone is not enough, which might surprise some people. No, Luke has more to tell us and the journey for those two disciples still has some way to go. As they come to the end of the road, the stranger who is with them, **'made as if to go on.'** The disciples though, still not knowing who he is, feel that they need his **presence** with them, so they ask him to stay. In other words they do not want him to go. It is now that something quite remarkable happens,

'While he was with them at table, he took the bread and said the blessing; then he broke it and handed it to them. And their eyes were opened and they recognised him.'

This is the moment when recognition finally comes because they recognise the **presence** of Jesus in the breaking of the bread. It is now during their meal together that they see who this stranger, they have been travelling with, really is, Jesus. Luke makes it clear, therefore, that the experience of the **presence** of Jesus in and through the Eucharist is also needed if we are to truly know who

Jesus actually is. Note now the response of those two disciples, **'They set out that instant and returned to Jerusalem,'** or their lives on recognising the **presence** of Jesus were completely transformed to the point that they had to go and tell others, **'There they found the Eleven assembled together with their companions, who said to them, 'Yes, it is true. The Lord has risen and has appeared to Simon. Then they told their story of what had happened on the road and how they had recognised him at the breaking of the bread.'**

Luke then highlights two experiences if we are to recognise today the **presence** of Jesus in our midst. Firstly, if we stay close to Jesus in the reading of the scriptures by reflecting on his life, his teaching, his death and his resurrection and if this penetrates our souls, then our hearts too will literally burn within us as we recognise his **presence** in our lives. Secondly, when we celebrate the Eucharist to recognise his **presence**, once again, in our lives as he strengthens us, upholds us and sustains us with his own body and blood. If we can recognise the **presence** of Jesus in our lives like this, it is then that through faith in him, his risen life grows in us.

In the dark times in which we live it is important for us to recognise the **presence** of Jesus, in our lives here and now. For he is **present** in the scriptures, please reach out to them and allow Jesus to speak to you and tell you how much you mean to him and how much he loves you. He is **present** in the Eucharist celebrated every day, throughout the whole world, for you and all those you love and care for. Finally, he is **present** in you and in your life of faith and love. Never forget that the Lord will never abandon you, for he is **present**, alive and active in your life now and always will be. For he is the God of hope, the God of love and above all the God of life. **He is Risen, He is Risen Indeed – Alleluia!**

Postscript

As I came to the end of this reflection I suddenly became aware of something and felt the need to add it here. I have highlighted the importance of the word **presence** in recognising how Jesus is truly **present** in our midst. That is to say the Risen Lord is truly **present** and active in our lives now. However, being the frail and weak human beings that we all are this is something that most of the time we either forget or take for granted. Yet during the recent period of lockdown some of us, perhaps, have had the time to reflect, on this truth of our faith, a little further and a little deeper

If we look carefully at the story of the disciples on their way to Emmaus a pattern begins to emerge, which may at first not seem obvious but when it is pointed out it certainly does. Look closely at the sequence of events and what do you find? Firstly, the **presence** of Jesus is to be found in the scriptures but this only becomes possible for the disciples when they recognise his **presence** in the Eucharist. Sounds familiar? Think about how we celebrate the Eucharist day-by-day, week-by-week and year-by-year, it is in fact an ancient tradition, which goes right back to the early days of the church and continues right up to the present day. Now what do we have? The liturgy of the word or in other words the reading of the scriptures through which we recognise the **presence** of God speaking to us comes first, followed by the celebration of the Eucharist in which we recognise the **presence** of his Son in his most precious body and blood. In other words it is exactly the same pattern that we find in Luke's description of the journey made by the disciples to Emmaus!

The simple but profound truth we can take from this is that God is truly **present** with us all as we make our own journeys through life. Sometimes we are aware of his **presence** but most of the time we are not but this does not change the truth of the promise he makes to all of us, **'I am with you always, to the end of the world.'** In these times of darkness, loneliness and great sadness for many people take heart from the fact that the Resurrected Lord is **present** in our midst, with his message of hope, life and love. All we have to do along with Thomas and those two disciples on the road to Emmaus is reach out and touch him.

'You believe because you can see me.

Happy are those who have not seen and yet believe.'

(John 20:29)

CHAPTER ELEVEN

Easter

'He has risen!'

Matthew 28:1-10

Reflecting back over the resurrection accounts that have come down to us through the gospels one of the features, which stands out, is the sheer despondency of the main characters. Whether it is the women on the way to the tomb with Mary Magdalene, the disciples on the road to Emmaus or the twelve who had literally locked themselves away in a room for fear of what might happen to them; they all appear to be in a state of utter devastation. Now of course this is completely understandable as their Lord and Master had just been crucified and buried in a tomb and with that, all their hopes and dreams for the future had died with him. Without Jesus they were all lost and alone, life now seemed to have no purpose or meaning any longer, all that remained were tears, sorrow and a deep sense of aching loss. Yet, perhaps, we need to look at their experiences in a new way and with fresh eyes. This description of how the early close followers of Jesus must have felt after losing him can, often, be our experience too. For many people life today is sad and lonely filled with feelings of isolation and even despair. God, as we have already said, can appear to be distant or even absent, leaving us with feelings of complete and utter loss. This, of course, serves to replicate those experiences of the early followers of Jesus as they stood in the dark and empty tomb completely bewildered as to what to do next. We have already said that Jesus bids us to come out of the darkness and into the light as he shares the power of his resurrection with us but for a moment let us stay in the tomb and in the darkness because this experience is important and we need to know why? Standing there with our feelings of sadness and deep sorrow reflecting how we might really be feeling right now, we need to realise something vitally important before we can take a step towards the light. That even in the darkness of the tomb we are not alone. No! For Christ is there with us, in the sadness, in the loneliness, in the anxiety, in the depression and yes even in the despair, we are not alone. Yet it does not end there for he is with us in the unhappiness, in the sorrow, in the sickness and yes, even in the death. For as we weep because of what life has done and perhaps continues to do to us, the truth is that God, through his Son, experiences these feelings with us too. Remember what we said on Good Friday about how he shares our pain so that we might share his life. Well this is where all of this happens, this is where all of it comes true because in the darkness of that tomb and therefore in the darkness of our own lives stands nothing less than the Risen Lord. Listen again to what he said, **'I have come that you may have life and have it to the full.'** (John 10:10) For all those who feel lost, lonely or afraid, for all those who feel that life is too much to bear, for all those who feel dead on the inside and that life has no meaning, purpose or value. Suddenly we discover the real meaning of Easter, that true life and therefore eternal life is to be found only in the risen Christ. Here in the darkness shines the light of his risen life and love and it banishes all our fears, worries and anxieties. '**Do not be afraid,**' (Matthew 28:10) he says to us before taking us by the hand and leading us out into the light.

This is why Easter must never been seen as something which took place exclusively in the past. Instead the Easter message challenges us to be energised, living as the people of the resurrection today with the risen Jesus being the source of our lives of faith. Once again we can say that the resurrection of the Son of God, changed and therefore transformed everything, nothing could, in fact, ever be the same again. The resurrected Christ is not only the source of our lives, filling us with his resurrected life but we are constantly being drawn closer and closer to him and this is true of the whole of creation if only we took the time to stop and look. The Christian then is invited by Christ to live a transformed life, in him, so that others may be touched by his grace, mercy and truth through us. Remember when we started off on our journey together and began with Lent, it seems such a long time ago now. However, at that point we identified three key areas of life to live by in our preparation for Easter,

1. *We must put self-interest to one side and instead focus our attention on the needs of others. We shall call this the selfless way of Christ.*

2. *To seek, as God's servant, only to do what is good.*

3. *To be dominated not by power, wealth and ambition but only by the love of God as revealed in his Son, Jesus Christ.*

Now, I hope, all of this makes sense because it is the way of Christ and it is our new way of living and being. This is the only way the world will ever be truly healed and God through his Son invites us to be part of it, sharing his life with us, so that we might share his life with others. This is why Easter is so full of joy and optimism because the Risen Christ has transformed everything, we are no longer in the darkness of the tomb because Jesus has **'unbound'** us and **'set us free.'** (John 11:44) In other words we have been changed from the inside out and now we can see that living in our midst is the resurrected Christ who gives both meaning and purpose to everything we do.

At the very heart of this book and the reason I have written it, is a very simple idea and that is to highlight and stress the importance of Jesus. The fundamental contention is that he, ultimately, is the source of everything. It is his life-giving Spirit, which energises our lives of faith and service because without him, therefore, we are truly lost. There is a danger that this central truth of our faith is being eroded and so whether it is the Church as an institution, if I can use that word, or us as individuals, we all need to literally, cling to Christ. Hence my primary motivation for writing this book was to help people understand '**The Real Meaning of Easter,**' which makes no sense whatsoever without Christ. When we look back at those early Christians we discover something exciting, how they were energised and transformed by the resurrection of Jesus because suddenly everything made sense. Life for them could not and would not ever be the same again. Yet, the same is equally true for us but only if we stay close to Jesus, then and only then will we, just like those early followers of the Lord, be able to live life in a new way by '**knowing him and the power of his resurrection.**' (Philippians 3:10)

So what then are the signs, in our lives, that we have ben energised, transformed and recreated by the power of his resurrection? How are we new creations in Christ? (2 Corinthians 5:17) The first thing that we need to call to mind is that there will always be a challenge and therefore a cost to discipleship, '**If anyone wants to be a follower of mine, let him renounce himself and take up his cross and follow me.**' (Matthew 16: 24) So with this in mind this how we know that we are living by and through the power of the risen Christ,

- That he is at the centre of our lives and of the communities we belong to.
- That we are called to be instruments of his mercy, compassion, forgiveness and love.

- That we can see, recognise and serve him in the rejected, despised, unwanted and unloved.

- That we can recognise him in his word (scripture) and that he invites us to enter into a conversation with him, which will be life changing.

- That he is present in our own experiences of life whether they be good or bad and that it is through recognising him there that he will change our lives.

- That he is present in the sacraments of the church to uphold and sustain us through life.

- That only in him is to be found the true meaning of all things, that he sets us free from Satan, Sin and Death and offers us eternal life.

- That we can do nothing without him but that we know, with certainty, that he is with us always and is the true source of our strength.

- That he shares his own life with us.

- That we can meet him in prayer and that he desires only what is good for us.

- That all suffering is a participation in the suffering of God.

- That by knowing and believing he shares his very life with us we can share that same life-giving, life-transforming, life with others.

Now this list is not meant to be exhaustive and you might like to add some of your own ideas but I am going to leave the last words to

Saint Paul who sums up perfectly the essence of Christian faith,

'For I am certain of this: neither death nor life, nor angels, nor principalities, nothing already in existence and nothing still to come, nor any power, nor the heights nor the depths, nor any created thing whatever, will be able to come between us and the love of God, known to us in Christ Jesus our Lord.' (Romans 8: 38-39)

If someone were to ask me to define, simply, the resurrection of Jesus and therefore to explain the real meaning of Easter, I would have to put it like this, 'Easter is when God revealed the power of His love for all people. Such love which came through the worst suffering imaginable, set us free from the power of Satan, Sin and Death, gave us the gift of new life here and now but also promised us eternal life with him.'

At the core of this book is a proposal, which is that everything needs to start from deep within us. At the core of our being is God, waiting for us; remember the 'God of Surprises?' All we have to do is let go and trust in him. You cannot get this from a book, it is something you have to feel and experience for yourself, that God loves **YOU**. If we learn to let go and simply place our trust in him, he will show us the way. If and I keep on using that word we can believe and trust that we are really loved by God, then that same love, the one that he has for us, the one that he revealed in the death and resurrection of his Son, the one that he gives to us as a free gift, will overflow out of our own hearts and into the lives of others because we will simply not be able to contain it! At this point we will know because we will have experienced that we are, in fact, nothing less than, **'a new creation.'** (2 Corinthians 17:5)

Let us now go back now, again, to that dark empty tomb we started this chapter with and have spoken so often about in this book and ask ourselves, 'what have we discovered?' That, in fact, we are not alone! 'Come out of the darkness, step into the light,' Christ says to us, **'Peace be with you.'** (John 20:19) Imagine that, after everything he had just been through, the sheer horror and degradation of the crucifixion and that by his own creation, God can still offer those wounded hands of friendship to his disciples and motivated only by pure love say, **'Peace be with you.'** Our reaction to this should be, with Saint John, to fall to our knees and say, **'My Lord and my God.'** (John 20: 28) Why is it then that some people fail to see this and that even people of faith sometimes lose sight of the resurrected Lord? The answer to this, perhaps, lies with the stone that sealed the tomb but equally blocks our minds and hardens our hearts. By being open to God the stone is removed, our minds are cleared and our hearts softened, as his resurrected love bursts out of the tomb and consumes us. Suddenly we see and believe that the light is stronger than any darkness that love is more powerful than any form of hate and that life really does triumph over death. The unselfish, self-sacrificial, unconditional love of God is like nothing the world had experienced before and it changed everything including creation itself. Such love consumes us and, in turn, invites us to be so caught up in it that it becomes a natural and therefore vital part of whom we are.

By living in such a way we are given a glimpse into eternity as we suddenly realise that God, in fact, lives through us. Now to live is to participate, that is to say '**Share in the Life of God,**' and as a result everything changes. Every face, every encounter, the scriptures, the sacraments, the church and the whole of creation are all alive and infused with his Risen Life. At the same time we can now also believe that we do, in fact, have nothing to fear, '**Do not be afraid,**' (Matthew 28:10) not even of death because love never dies. The darkness of that tomb has been shattered by resurrected love, a love that has been shared with us until the end of time itself. This is our faith. Faith, in the resurrected Jesus, which upholds and sustains us as we journey through life for in his words, '**I am with you always; yes, to the end of time.**' (Matthew 28: 20)

'There is no need for you to be afraid. I know who you are looking for Jesus, who was crucified. He is not here, for he has risen, as he said he would.' (Matthew 28)

CHAPTER TWELVE
Easter

'Do not let your hearts be troubled'
John 14: 1-12

As we journey deeper and deeper into the real meaning of Easter a thought struck me that I would like to share with you. I have often found myself reflecting on how wonderful it would have been to be present with Jesus when he spoke with his disciples. There are those moments in the gospels when Jesus becomes very intimate with them, when he opens his heart to the twelve by describing his relationship with his Father and how he desires that we share in that relationship too. There are other occasions when it becomes clear that Jesus not only knows the hidden depths of the disciples but he also knows the secret places of our hearts too. This can be the cause of great comfort and consolation when times are hard and this is exactly the point. We are not meant to stay in the darkness of the tomb; this is not the real meaning of Easter at all. No! Christ calls us out into the light and when we do feel that our lives have been broken and life has become too much to bear he simply says, **'Do not let your hearts be troubled. Trust in God still, and trust in me.'**

In his 'Spiritual Exercises,' Saint Ignatius of Loyola encourages participants to engage in what he calls 'imaginative contemplation' of the gospel scene. Take, for example, the gospel reading we are now reflecting on, **John 14: 1-12**, does it take place at night or during the day? Are Jesus and the disciples in a quiet place by themselves? Are they in doors or outside? How are they dressed and what does each of the characters look like? To do this we need to read the whole of the gospel passage and then by using our imagination place ourselves directly in the scene. Let us say the whole incident takes place at night in the foothills, somewhere in Galilee. It is dark and there is a small fire around which Jesus and his disciples are gathered, now place yourself alongside the twelve and allow yourself to be absorbed into the scene. The night is chilly and the small fire, as it burns, crackles and spits throwing out a warm and gentle heat, which you can feel on your face. Perhaps the disciples are a little subdued and so are you, everyone is feeling down and troubled and there is an atmosphere of tension. Look at the faces of the twelve, eavesdrop on their conversation, what are they saying? Why are they so afraid? Then you pick up on something, which literally grabs your attention. One of them mentions a concern that they all have been thinking about but were too afraid to ask and that is, Jesus is going to leave them and it will be soon. This is why there is uneasiness about the disciples. They had been with Jesus for a little over two years now. He had been their constant companion and the source of their faith. It was for him that they had literally dropped everything, home, family and employment. If then Jesus was to leave them, what were they to do because without him they would be lost? Can you experience their anxiety at this point and make it your own? Can you imagine what life would have been like for the disciples without Jesus? Perhaps as you read this you feel distant from Jesus too, as if he is absent, not present, in your life as well? It is really important, at this stage, to recognise and value our own experiences of life and faith, whether they are positive or negative. Because this then makes us one with the disciples as they gathered around the flames of that tiny fire with Jesus still in their midst. All of them are on the edge of, perhaps, being overwhelmed by a great sadness at the thought of Jesus not being with them anymore.

Now we have to focus our attention on Jesus. Look at his face, what does he look like? His eyes are moving from one disciple to the next as he picks up on exactly how they are feeling. Then his eyes focus exclusively on you and you become aware that he knows, in the most intimate detail, all of your concerns, worries and anxieties. How does this make you feel now? It is at this point that, somehow, you know that Jesus understands the fears of all those present, including you. That he knows they fear being parted from him and so he wants to reassure them by speaking directly to their hearts, **'Do no let your hearts be troubled. Trust in God; trust also in me.'** What does his voice sound like and how does it make you feel? Stay with this for a while and imagine Jesus is talking directly to you. His wish is to reassure you bringing comfort, consolation and hope.

What happens next borders on being unbelievable because the like of which has never been said before, '**I am going now to prepare a place for you, and after I have gone and prepared you a place, I shall return to take you with me; so that where I am you may be too.**' So Jesus is leaving them then, it is true, and all their anxieties were warranted. Death, it seems would take him from them and they would be left alone. Yet, Jesus is also, in these words, reassuring them and in turn us that not even death can destroy the bonds of love that have been made between them. Moreover, one day they will be together again!

Perhaps the disciples have not really been listening to what Jesus said. Instead on receiving confirmation that he will be leaving them they are on the edge of being completely overwhelmed by their fear. At the very least they are confused and fail to understand what everything means. Without Jesus what can they do? They had placed all their hope and all their trust him. He was the one who had inspired them and yet now, here he was, talking of leaving. It was impossible for them to imagine what life would be like for them without Jesus, their Lord and Master, in their midst. Have you ever experienced such feelings, the absence of God or the fear of the absence of God? It is perfectly acceptable to admit such anxiety, after all this is exactly why this gospel passage has come to us.

At this point Thomas, on behalf of the twelve, speaks up and to do that he must be brutally honest, '**Lord, we do not know where you are going, so how can we know the way?**' This is exactly why, if we are to grow in our faith, then we must be totally honest too in the way we feel when it comes to our own worries and anxieties. Remember that growth in faith is something to be experienced from the inside out and here we have living proof of that process in action. Thomas is simply telling it straight, something, which comes from the inside and represents how all of the disciples are actually feeling at that point, **'Lord, we do not know where you are going, so how can we know the way?'**

What Jesus says next is both astounding and stunning, to say the least, and should make the hairs on the back of our necks stand up, **'I am the Way, The Truth and the Life. No one can come to the Father except through me.'** In other words it is through Jesus that you will experience the Father and it is by following him that you will be led to the Father. Only then by following in the footsteps of Jesus will you find both **Truth** and **Life**. Jesus will lead the way, we are invited to follow and our destination is the Father.

At this point it is Philip who speaks up, perhaps reflecting confusion as to what exactly Jesus means by the Father. After all we need to keep in mind that for the Jew and remember Jesus and all his disciples were Jews, God was the supreme creator of everything and sustained the entire universe and all things in it. So with this in mind Philip says, **'Lord, let us see the Father and then we shall be satisfied.'** It is in reply to this question that Jesus leaves no room for ambiguity as to his true identity because his words are stunning and breath-taking,

'Have I been with you all this time, Philip and you still do not know me? To have seen me is to have seen the Father.'

At this point Jesus is inviting the twelve to put everything together, the entire time they have been with one another and see, perhaps, for the very first time who Jesus actually is. His life of pure goodness, his mercy, compassion, forgiveness and love for all people but especially for the rejected, despised, unwanted and unloved. All this, his words and all his actions have made the Father visible for all too see. This is because the Father is the source of all that is good and therefore of all love and this is what Jesus came to reveal because in him is to be found nothing less than the reality of God, **'I am in the Father and the Father is in me.'**

At Easter Jesus beckons us out of the tomb, 'do not stay in the darkness,' and calls us into the light. However, he knows full well that we can be fearful so he says, **'Do not let your hearts be troubled, trust in God still and trust in me.'** In the world he invites us to walk in his footsteps so that others may see the light of his love in us. Dedicated to him and enlivened by his Holy Spirit we are called to live lives that show something of his mercy, compassion, forgiveness and love for all people but especially those who are rejected, despised, unwanted and unloved. To strengthen and sustain us on our journey he gently tells us, **'I am going to prepare a place for you....... In my Father's house ...... so that where I am you may be too.'** His final parting gift for us, is to never forget a truth written deep into our hearts, **'To have seen me is to have seen the**

Father.'

Easter then is the great Christian feast, which marks the change and therefore the transformation of everything. It leaves no doubt as to whom Jesus is but the truth of the resurrection must live in us too. In the gospel passage we have just explored Jesus essentially tells us, not to be afraid but to place all our hope and all our trust in him. By staying close to Christ, by loving and serving those in need, others might just be able to catch a glimpse of the resurrected Christ in us because he and therefore the Father is the source of all that is good.

CHAPTER THIRTEEN

The Ascension

'And I am with you always, to the very end of the age'

Matthew 28: 16-20

If we spend any length of time reflecting on the gospels then we cannot help but be anything less than impressed by their brutal honesty. Jesus has spent forty days with his disciples after his resurrection from the dead. He has taught them many things and performed deeds that they could not explain. He knows that, at times, they have struggled to believe and make sense out of everything that has happened but now has come the time for him to leave them. The eleven are told to go back to Galilee, to the mountain where they would meet him for the last time. On seeing him Matthew tells us, **'they worshipped him,'** however, he also goes on to say remarkably, **'but some doubted him.'** For us today this almost borders on being unbelievable. After all they had seen and heard some of them still doubted! They saw him die on the cross, witnessed him being buried in the tomb and believed then that it was, literally, all over. All their hopes and dreams for the future had been crushed but then everything changed because he was, in fact, alive. Once again they could speak with him, eat with him, laugh and cry with him. Once again he could make their **'hearts**

burn within them,' as he explained the meaning of the scriptures. They could reach out and touch his wounds and see that death could not hold him and yet, despite all of this, doubts still remained in some of their hearts and minds. What Matthew is doing here is being honest. In the early days of the Christian church there were some who struggled to believe and whose faith was therefore weak. After all it must have been very difficult to grasp the meaning and significance of everything that had happened, especially in the light of Jesus's immanent departure. Matthew wants us to know this and that doubt is a natural part of being human. After all remember Thomas who refused to believe that Jesus had risen from the dead unless he could physically touch the wounds in the actual flesh of Christ, made by the nails? Equally though and this is something we have consistently made clear in our journey into the real meaning of Easter we should not and therefore cannot let our lives be dominated by fear.

So yet again, what Matthew is trying to make abundantly clear, and it is the core proposal of this book, is that, we must be able and willing to place all of our hope and all of our trust in Jesus. If we fail to do this then we become lost and our faith falters. As a result let us now see what happens next when, **'Jesus approached them.'** In other words he sees them and he comes to them, he draws near to them because he knows how much they need him. He has made it clear to them who he is, **'I and the Father are one, to have seen me is to have seen the Father, to have heard me is to have heard** the Father,' but now he goes on to say, 'All authority in heaven and earth has been given to me.' So yet again he is inviting them to place all their trust in him, 'Trust in God, Trust also in me.' (John 14:1) Now though he is going to place his trust in them and in turn us by revealing to the disciples their mission, 'Go, therefore, and make disciples of all nations; baptise them in the name of the Father and of the Son and of the Holy Spirit, and teach them to observe all the commands I gave you.' It would appear that Jesus is being quite detailed and specific in what he is asking them to do in so far as their first and therefore primary objective is to, 'make disciples of all nations.' This means, of course, disciples of Jesus and this, in turn, brings us right back to our main contention that Jesus is quite simply, everything.

At this moment I want to pause and highlight something, which can be easily lost as we focus all of our attention on the Ascension. Why did Jesus ask the disciples to meet him in Galilee? Matthew is very specific about this point, 'Meanwhile the eleven disciples set out for Galilee, to the mountain where Jesus had arranged to meet them.' I do not believe that the meeting took place in Galilee purely by chance and it would be there that Jesus would both commission the disciples and leave them. Instead I would suggest that there is a direct connection between what Jesus said to the eleven and the meaning of where it took place. If they are to 'make disciples, baptise, teach and observe all the commands' of Jesus then what better place to remind them of what this all meant than Galilee? It was in Galilee that Jesus left the banks of the river Jordan and went in search of all those people who had been told that they were not wanted by God, we have called them the rejected, despised, unwanted and unloved. He then assured them of two things, not only that the Father loved them but that they would be first in the Kingdom of Heaven. Jesus now, on that mountain, wanted the disciples to remember this and make it their mission too. It was in Galilee that Jesus performed many of his miracles, healing the sick, restoring sight to the bind, curing lepers and raising the dead. It was in Galilee that Jesus offered comfort and consolation to those who mourn, to the widow, to the poor, to the orphan, to the broken hearted and to the destitute. It was in Galilee that Jesus fed the hungry, climbed the hill and through the beatitudes turned the values of the world upside down. It was in Galilee that Jesus first clashed with the Pharisees speaking out on behalf of those who had no voice, those who were powerless and all those who lived on the margins. It was in Galilee that Jesus made it abundantly clear by quoting the prophet Hosea that what God the Father wanted most was, '**Mercy, not sacrifice.**' (Matthew 9:13; Hosea 6:6) This is the Gospel, the good news that they are now to proclaim to the whole world. This is their commission, to place all their hope and all their trust in him and to '**Go, therefore, and make disciples of all nations.**' All those memories of the time that they had spent together would have come flooding back to the eleven as they stood on that mountain, with Jesus, in Galilee and that is why he specifically chose the location of their last meeting. Now they knew, now they finally understood, even though some of them had doubts and of course Jesus knew that. You see he chose them, warts and all as they say. He knew that they would not be perfect, he knew that there would be times when they would stumble and fall and yet he still chose now to place his trust in them. All that they had to do was to stay close to him and incarnate, that is to say, realise or make present his presence in the world.

Of course the mission Jesus gives to his disciples is the same mission he gives to his church and in turn to us today. We like them are invited and therefore called by Christ to, **'make disciples of all nations.'** If we are ever going to achieve this then we have to, first and foremost, stay close to him and this means learning as much as we possibly can about Jesus. Secondly it is not enough just to learn about him but in our own way and through our own lives we have to learn to live like him. This means having a passionate commitment to the dispossessed and all those living on the margins, the rejected, despised, unwanted and unloved. Just like him we have to be instruments of God's mercy, compassion, forgiveness and love. Just like him we have to become servants of one another recognising the absolute dignity of every human being. Just like him we have to be willing to put self-interest to one side, seek only to do good and reject any obsession with wealth, power, status or ambition. Just like him we have to strive to be better human beings by seeking the way that leads to truth, justice and peace. Just like him our calling is to try to make the world in which we live a better place for all people. Living in this way allows us to **'Share in the Life of God,'** because it is not our own Gospel or good news that we are offering to the world but his. However, the one thing we must never forget is that we do none of these things alone or through our own strength, rather he has promised to be always with us, **'And look, I am with you always; yes, to the end of time.'** These are the tender words of Christ offered to both his disciples then and to us now. He knows our weakness, he knows that we will face persecution, rejection and hardship, he knows that we will stumble and fall but equally he assures us that he will never leave us, even when our numbers are few.

This then is our calling, this is Jesus's invitation to us and that includes you and me, to continue his mission and to be his presence in the world. For the simple truth is that Christ lives in and through his Church, which is why Saint Paul defined it as **'the body of Christ.'** (Romans 12:5) In these parting words of Jesus to his disciples in the familiar environment of Galilee he tells them and in turn us what his vision for the Church actually is. Yet there is still one more gift he has to offer but they will have to wait another ten days for that. What we can say here though as we reach the very edges of our journey into the real meaning of Easter is that the risen Christ will not leave his Church and therefore his people alone. No! What he will do is pour into it his life giving Spirit and it is this, which will enable it to continue with his mission to transform the world. When we realise this suddenly everything changes because we are able to recognise both in our own lives and in the communities to which we belong that Christ lives. His mercy, His compassion, His forgiveness and above His love continues not just in the life of the Church but also in **YOU**!

CHAPTER FOURTEEN

Pentecost

'As the Father has sent me, I am sending you.'

John 20: 19-23

We are now coming to the end of our **'Journey into The Real Meaning of Easter.'** It has been fifty days since the resurrection of Jesus from the dead and, once again, we come across the disciples in a room, **'with the doors locked,'** because they were afraid. Jesus comes to them with the reassuring words, **'Peace be with you!'** and **'shows them his hands and his side.'** Immediately, **'The disciples were overjoyed when they saw the Lord.'** At this point Jesus repeats his greeting to them, **'Peace be with you.'** We now need to pause and reflect on what has happened so far and why Jesus says the same thing twice to his disciples. Once again, it is the presence of Jesus in the midst of his closest followers, which serves to comfort and reassure them. It is his presence, which fills them with his peace whilst at the same time their hearts are **'overjoyed.'** This then is what the presence of Jesus actually does bringing peace and joy to those who follow him. Yet now there must be a change in them because the promise he made to them that he, **'would be with them always,'** is about to come true but, perhaps, not in the way they had expected. We are now reaching the most crucial point in our journey into the real meaning of Easter. Jesus has a task for them, and in turn us to perform and upon this everything will depend. You see as Jesus stands in their midst he knows that their mission and the mission of the church, which begins at Pentecost, will be nothing less, than to make him present in the world.

What Jesus says next though is quite remarkable, '**As the Father has sent me, I am sending you.**' In other words their mission in the world is to be exactly the same as that of Jesus. What Jesus received from the Father, so do his followers, it is as simple as that. Yet these words of Christ should make us both 'shudder' and 'tremble' as they are so, literally, awesome. The only task the disciples, the church and in turn us are called to perform is to be the presence of Jesus in the world! Notice that he does not tell them what they have to do or where they are to go; this is something that guided by the grace of the Holy Spirit they can work out for themselves later. No! The only thing that matters is being the presence of Jesus in the world and this mission comes directly from him who was, himself, sent by the Father.

They, and we in our turn, now know what this mission is because we have seen and heard it so many times before in our journey into the real meaning of Easter. Go to all people but especially the rejected, despised, unwanted and unloved and assure them of two things,

- *That they are loved conditionally by God.*
- *That they will be first in the Kingdom of Heaven.*

To achieve this you must be instruments of his,

- *Mercy*
- *Compassion*
- *Forgiveness*
- *Justice*
- *Love*

Jesus has shown them the way; he has, in his life and ministry, revealed what it means to be truly human and in so doing revealed the potential for humanity. As they look at Jesus they are reminded of the cost or the price paid by God to realise the presence of his Kingdom in the world. They can see the wounds, once again, of the cross still borne in his body and so can recall his words to them and in turn to us, **'If anyone wants to be a follower of mine, let him renounce himself and take up his cross and follow me.'** (Matthew 16:24) Of course, there will be a cost to discipleship but that is what being a follower of Jesus really means and it is the only way the world can be transformed. If it cost him everything it might just cost us the same too!

Jesus knows, as we have already seen, that they are weak and sometimes their faith in him fails. They cannot perform the task he has given them alone, they simply do not have the strength. So he will keep his promise to them by **'being with them always, even to**

the end of the age.' (Matthew 28:20) What happens next needs to be given careful consideration because everything depends on it and at the same time also involves us. Jesus is fully aware that they can do nothing without him but he also knows that his presence with them must change if they are to truly realise his mission for them in the world. As a result he will give them his own Spirit, which will energise and enable them to complete the task he has entrusted to them. This now is a unique moment in the Gospels because it will recall the origins of our creation. The actions performed by Jesus now, therefore, are quite deliberate. However, let us first note what he does not do. He does not touch them in the way he healed the sick and secondly he does not bless them in the way in which he taught the people about the Father. Instead, **'He breathed on them and said: 'Receive the Holy Spirit.'** Now why is this so important? For us to understand the true significance of what Jesus is doing here we need to go back to the book of Genesis and to creation itself,

'God shaped man from the soil of the ground and blew the breath of life into his nostrils, and man became a living being.' (Genesis 2:7)

So just as God breathed life into humanity, shaped from the dust of the ground, in the same way Jesus breathed life into his disciples, the church and in turn, us. The important thing for us to note here is that without God there would be no life in humanity. It is His Spirit, which animates, or gives life, to that which was originally nothing but soil or dust. This then is what makes us both human and alive. It is this same Holy Spirit, the Spirit of the living God that Jesus breathes into the disciples giving them His life and making them truly human. It is this same Spirit Jesus breathes into the church and in turn us, giving us life too. We live, therefore, only because of him, as it is His Spirit, which dwells in us.

At this point we are almost coming full circle and yet this is exactly the point that we were always destined to meet on a journey into the real meaning of Easter. You see, as we have consistently maintained, everything is and has to be about Jesus. Saint Paul understood this all too well when he said, **'yet it is no longer I who live, but Christ, who lives in me.'** (Galatians 2:20) This book could not have been written without Jesus, not a single word or sentence could have been put down on paper without him, which for me is a fact! My primary motivation for writing this book was to highlight the importance of Jesus both in the life of the church and in our own lives too. The disciples understood this that is why they did not want Jesus to leave them but Jesus understood this too that is why he promised to be with them **'until the end of the age.'** However, what is also true is that we are also weak and sometimes try to depend too much on our own strength, something, which Jesus guards us against. To counter this we need to constantly call to mind that it is only the Spirit of the living Christ, which makes us truly alive. When we recognise this and can become totally dependent on it, then just as with the disciples we will be, **'filled with joy.'** However, when we fail to recognise our utter dependency on the Living Lord, we lose strength, we stumble and fall and become lost in the darkness, which threatens to overwhelm us. When this happens the church and our lives stay in the shadows of the tomb, the very place we are not meant to be. The further we move away from Jesus the more we become lost in the ways of the world and the more we justify this, then the more corrupt we become. Jesus on the other hand bids us to come out of the darkness and into the light. The Risen Lord stands with us pouring His Holy Spirit into our hearts. We have one task, one mission, to be his presence in the world and this should fill our hearts with joy. Others now should be able to recognise this in us too; lives renewed and sustained by Christ. This life-giving spirit given to us by God in and through His Son will energise us into action as we hear again his one and only commandment, **'I give you a new commandment; love one another, just as I have loved you. It is by your love for one another, that everyone will recognise you as my disciples.'** (John 13: 34) It seems amazing that it all comes down to this but it does. The cost was great but it revealed the depth of God's love for humanity. What is even more amazing is that when we love like that, we make him present in the world today and it is this, which enables us to do nothing less than, **'Share in the Life of God.'**

Out of the darkness of the tomb overflows the light of God's love

'Now go and do the same yourself' (Luke 10:37)

Some Final Thoughts

I found myself writing much of this book during the Coronavirus (Covid-19) pandemic of 2020. This, of course, involved a lockdown confining most people to their homes, which also coincided with Easter. Not being able to physically attend church services during Holy Week caused great pain for many Christians. However, I used the time to make my own journey into the real meaning of Easter and this book is the fruit of my labour. Being alone meant that I could focus my attention on God at a deeper level by immersing myself in the scriptures and reflecting on what they were saying to humanity during this time of crisis. To me it felt very much like we had all entered the darkness of the tomb with him together and waited there for something to happen. For many people it seemed like God was silent, absent and distant from the cries of his people. The darkness of the tomb threatened to overwhelm many under a tidal wave of despair. Yet my journey taught me an important lesson that God, in fact, never stops talking to his people, never leaves us alone and whatever pain, misery and suffering we go through God shares too.

Easter is that moment when the tomb bursts open and the light consumes the darkness and what emerges is not just life but eternal life. Hope puts pay to despair, love defeats hate and death is vanquished forever. It is important for me that I actually believe everything that I write because I am sharing with you aspects of my own intimate relationship with God. I have made it clear all the way through the pages of this book that we can meet God in our own experiences of life. Unless, therefore, I have done this for myself I cannot offer it with any degree of integrity or sincerity to anybody else. You see I believe in a God who, motivated only by love, comes in search of us, knowing that we are suffering and in desperate need of healing. I believe that this God expresses that love in and through the life, death and resurrection of his Son Jesus Christ. I further believe that there is, literally, nothing that this God is not prepared to do for us and this includes suffering and dying a shameful and humiliating death. In this way our experiences becomes God's experiences and this is how we can share directly in the life of God. Anything, which threatens to separate us from the love of God, as revealed in his Son, is defeated and this ultimately means Satan, Sin and Death. This is why Jesus never grows tired of saying, **'Do not be afraid.'** (Matthew 14:27)

Going back then to the darkness of that tomb we all entered, Christ invites us to come out and stand in the light of his love. The resurrection of Christ changes everything the whole of creation was transformed by his all-embracing and redeeming love. Yet the fundamental truth of this is that in every moment and in every second of our lives now we cannot only experience this resurrected love but we can be transformed by it. Ultimately the Good News is that God is never absent but only present, closer to us than we could ever begin to imagine and when the darkness does threaten to overwhelm us all we have to do is reach out and touch him. For he is there in the depths of our own hearts and he is there in the kindness and the love of others and when we realise this we are truly, **'Sharing in the life of God.'**

And Finally

One of my ambitions in writing a book like this is to encourage everyone to do theology. Most people's immediate reaction to this is to associate theology with the clergy or with academics. In fact nothing could be further from the truth. This is because whenever we seek to make sense out of our own lives or the lives of the families and communities to which we belong, in relation to God, we are doing theology. Whenever we seek to make sense out suffering humanity again in relation to God, we are doing theology. This is because theology, by way of definition, is simply our striving to make sense out of God and our relationship with him. Where then does this process begin? It starts with our own experiences and our own lives, just like that treasure hidden in a field, waiting to be discovered because the kingdom of heaven is within **YOU.**

Sean Loone

Pentecost 2020

THANK YOU

First and foremost I want to thank the people, parish and school of Our Lady of the Wayside without whom this book and indeed all three books in the series would not have been possible. Now I would like to thank some specific people starting with Fr. Gerry Murray the parish priest of Our Lady of the Wayside when I first arrived. I thank Fr. Gerry for believing in me and supporting my candidacy for the diaconate it became a huge turning point in my life. Next I thank Fr. Louis McRaye, sadly no longer with us, for his wise words and council as I prepared for ordination. No one who spent time in the presence of this holy man could not help but feel that he had been sent to us from God. I now need to acknowledge the role of Creina Hearn not just in my own life but also in the life of the parish as a whole. For her consistent support, dedication, devotion and faith to Christ, His Church and His people in this place a huge and well-deserved, 'thank you.' My ordination, which took place at Our Lady of the Wayside was one of the most defining moments in my life, an experience I will never forget. One of the things about the ordination service itself, which has continued to linger long in my memory and in my heart was the music. For that I owe a huge debt of gratitude to Helena Madden and her music team. I have for a number of years had a close association with the school at Our Lady of the Wayside

School getting to know both children and staff very well. I am always amazed at their dedication, work ethic and commitment to the faith. Hence, I would like to take this opportunity to thank the Head Teacher, Mr Ben Taylor for continuing to believe in me and in my ministry to the school. I worked with Fr. Gerardo Fabrizio for seven years in the parish and throughout that time he constantly offered me not only his support but shared with me his considerable experience and wisdom. He had the knack of asking me the most difficult of questions, largely based on scripture, whenever I was invited to give talks to the parish, thanks for that Father! The current priest Father Andrew Franklin continues to support, encourage and challenge me in my ministry all of which I value and appreciate very much. I would also like to mention Father Peter Hawkins who for many years was my mentor and remains a close friend, one who, in fact, is never afraid to 'tell it me straight!' Finally, when it comes to priests there is one I need to thank even though I never actually met him and that is Father Paddy O'Mahony, a man who dedicated most of his priestly life to the people and the parish. His vision was to be part of a worshipping community that never forgot, for one moment, its obligation to serve the poor and needy of the world. This is why I decided to donate all of the profits from the sale of this book to the trust set up, after his death, in his name, to continue the work he so passionately believed in as an essential part of being the church, as the body of Christ, in the world today. Our Lady of the Wayside is a special place, filled with special people, there are in fact, literally, too many of them for me to mention. Yet the simple truth is that without them this book would never have been written. For that reason at the end of the book you will find greater detail about the Church building and what it means to the people of the parish. In a book about the resurrection though the simple truth is that Easter has to be experienced because God desires that he shares his very life with us. It is the people that make the church, it is the people that make the difference and it is through the people of God that Easter and the resurrection can be experienced. So, once again, I thank the people, the parish and the school of Our Lady of the Wayside for all you have given and continue to give to me. May God bless you, now and always?

Deacon Sean Loone

January 2021

POSTSCRIPT

OUR LADY OF THE WAYSIDE

In all of my books, so far, I have tried to stress the importance of the role played by the parish Church of Our Lady of the Wayside in both my ministry and in my own personal life of faith. So as I come to the end of my final book in the series I wanted to say a little bit more about the Church itself for all those who have asked for greater detail. To this end, I would love to have included photographs but unfortunately the cost involved has made this impossible. However, I would refer readers to the parish web site at ourladyofthewaysidechurchshirley.co.uk, where you can find a number of illustrations, which I hope will bring to life what I now have to say about the Church building itself.

Construction of the Church began in 1965 directly after The Second Vatican Council ended. Without going into too much detail the Council completely changed the way in which Catholics worshipped by emphasising how Christ is, actually, present in the midst of the worshipping community. Our Lady of the Wayside Church clearly expresses this new approach in both its design and build. However, the original Church, now the parish hall, was built in 1937 but the growing Catholic population in the area required something on a grander scale to meet its need and by its completion in 1966 this was clear for everyone in the area to see.

The architect was a local man by the name of Brian Rush and Our Lady of the Wayside was to be one of his earliest projects. He was helped in this process by the then parish priest one Father Paddy O'Mahony who was to remain in charge of the parish until 1991. I think it is fair to say that he was a larger than life character but hugely inspirational to all those who knew him and a man who definitely knew what he wanted. Hence he worked closely with Mr Rush in his plans to bring to life, in a physical and tangible form, the vision of the Second Vatican Council for God's people in Shirley.

Now let us move on and explore the Church building itself. To get the most out of any visit to the parish Church of Our Lady of the Wayside it is best to enter the building through the main entrance located on the Stratford Road. Immediately you find yourself in a light filled Narthex or Porch. One of the first things you cannot help but notice is the abundance of plants to be found there. This is quite deliberate and is a main feature of the Church symbolising life and growth both in the natural world but equally also in our own lives of faith. On the left hand side, as you enter through the large glass doors, is a picture of Fr. O'Mahony and list of all those people who, in the early days, gave so generously to equip and beautify the new

Church. As we pass the day chapel, again on the left hand side, we come across a piece of art which has proved to be so influential in my own life of faith that of **'The Crucified Christ,'** built directly into the brick wall. It is stunning in both its simplicity and beauty and I would urge any visitor to take the time to reflect on its profound faith-filled meaning. The creator was a local artist, Walter Ritchie, based in Kenilworth. It was this very image, which inspired me to write the book, **'Only in the Crucified God – Questions and Answers on Faith, Hope and Love.'** If you have the time it is also worthwhile, at this point, popping into the day chapel where you will find a life-sized framed sketch of **'The Crucified Christ,'** presented as a gift by the artist to Fr. O'Mahony. By the main door of the Church you will also find a striking sculpture of a murdered dove entitled, **'Peace in Our Time.'** This was given to Fr. O'Mahony by its sculptor Angelo Bordonari, in tribute to his well-known work for justice and peace.

Now let us turn our attention to the right hand side of the Narthex as you enter the Church from the Stratford Road. Here you cannot help but notice the baptistery. At its heart is the font, made out of Portland stone, situated on what looks like a small island surrounded by flowing water. Carved on the side of the font are images from God's creation both human and animal. The whole of the baptistery is encased with stained and painted glass designed by Tom Fairs. The aim is to depict in three pivotal scenes, moments in history when God intervened to save his people.

1. *The Passover of the Old Testament – seen in the symbols of the desert, a pillar of fire and the sea.*

2. *The saving actions of Christ in the New Testament – seen in the tomb/womb, the cross and the gifts of the Holy Spirit.*

3. *The Resurrection – seen in a flash of light and energy along with the five wounds of Christ.*

Around the font, itself, is to be found a swirling cascade of running water, which reminds us of the living, life-filled water of baptism through which those who are baptised are given new life by Christ. Finally, behind the font but built into the fabric of the baptistery is a holder for the Paschal (Easter) Candle, a symbol of the Risen Christ, the Light of the world.

To complete our journey through the Narthex, opposite the baptistery you will find the Day Chapel. This is most often used for weekday masses for small groups. It does, however, afford a full view of the main church through a large window and has linked speakers so that families with young children can use it, if they wish, during the Sunday services. Around the walls of the Day Chapel can be found a variety of scenes, depicted in stained glass, reflecting on the various stages of life from birth to death. It is a place where you can sit down and be quiet, perhaps, spending time in silent prayer and reflection. At the Maundy Thursday Mass the Blessed Sacrament is reserved here and it becomes a place of devotion where the faithful can spend time with Christ on the night he was betrayed.

As we leave the Narthex we enter the main body of the Church through rather large sliding glass doors, which again serve to make everything as transparent as possible for the faithful. At this point it is worthwhile standing still for a while to take in the large space you are confronted with. Your eyes will inevitably be drawn to the huge figure of the **'Risen Christ,'** which dominates this area, designed by Dame Elizabeth Frink 1930-993, one of the most famous women sculptors of the century. Once again, as with Brian Rush this must have been one of her earlier pieces of work. She was given the challenging task of showing the **'Risen Christ'** who greeted the apostles and disciples after the Resurrection in a body somehow recognisably the same but in some mysterious way different, bearing the five wounds of the Passion. It is said that viewed from the left we can see the more Jewish aspects of Christ with a beard, whereas from the right he is seen more like someone from the Greek world wearing the laurel crown of victory. The New Testament especially in the writings of John and Paul represents Jesus from the Greek and the Hebrew points of view. All of this seeks to reveal that the God of Jesus Christ is the God who includes everyone and excludes no one. His victory over Satan, Sin and Death and his bursting forth from the tomb is something he shares with all people, for all time. This wonderful image of Christ still bearing the wounds of his crucifixion, yet coming in search of us, to find us, simply because he loves us, is what inspired me to write this book.

Below the statue of the **'Risen Christ'** we see the large altar made of a single block of Portland stone weighing no less than seven tons! On the front is inscribed words from both the Old and the New Testaments, **'I will pour out my spirit on all flesh,'** a reference, once again, to God leaving no one out; the lettering was, incidentally, carved by Walter Ritchie the man who also created the **'Crucified Christ'** in the Narthex. To the left and right of the altar stand two large ceramic altar candlesticks, made locally in Henley in Arden.

Behind the altar and growing up the wall towards the natural diffused light coming in above the sanctuary are many different types of plants, with their different texture and shape, first encountered in the Narthex. Once again we are reminded of the challenge given to us by Christ to grow constantly in our faith, never standing still but always on the move towards a greater love of him and of each other. The altar itself is positioned both carefully and deliberately so that the congregation is gathered on three sides creating a very real sense of community sharing together in the worship of the parish. In fact close to four hundred people can be accommodated very close to the sanctuary. At the back of the church is a gallery complete with cantilevered supports, useful for special occasions and the great festivals and solemnities when the Church is particularly crowded.

If you now stand on the sanctuary steps with your back to the altar and look right then high up on the wall you will find a beautiful icon of Mary holding her Son, Jesus. This stunning image portrays Mary as the mother of God and was commissioned by the then parish priest Fr. Gerardo Fabrizio to commemorate the fiftieth anniversary of the Church. If you now take the time to look left you will be able to spot the Lady Chapel with its beautiful carved figure of Mary holding her Son close as she gazes out across the church. It was carved from a single block of teak wood by Walter Ritchie and depicts Mary clasping to her breast the naked and vulnerable Christ child. Just like the image of the **'Crucified Christ'** in the Narthex this remarkable work of art deserves to be treated with dignity, respect and devotion as it draws us deeply into the Gospel narrative of the God who, once again, comes in search of us. The humility of 'Mother and Child,' of humanity and divinity found in this image eventually became the inspiration for my first book, **'Born for Us – A Journey into the Real Meaning of Christmas.'** Carved into the brickwork behind 'Mother and Child' is a line from a poem by Gerard Manley Hopkins SJ, **'Men are meant to share her life as does air, if I have understood, she holds, high motherhood.'** Finally, if you look carefully behind the side altar in the Lady Chapel you will see some stained and painted glass by Tom Fairs, which suggests by its shapes and colours fruits, recalling Mary, Mother of God, as honoured in the prayer, **'Blessed is the fruit of thy womb, Jesus,'** (Luke 1:42) and the fruits of the Holy Spirit as described by Saint Paul in his letter to the Galatians. (Galatians 5:22)

Looking at the Church as a whole, natural materials are used in a simple and pleasing way; brick for the walls, glass for the windows, stone for the sanctuary, wood for the floor and ceiling. The effect is to make everything as transparent as possible. As a result from the inside you can catch glimpses of the outside world, whilst on the outside you can catch glimpses of what takes place within. The effect is for the Church to be a conduit connecting the world with God's people by offering a place where not only worship can happen but where everyone is made to feel welcome. In many ways it reminds me of the painting, **'The Last Supper,'** by the artist Salvador Dali, which serves to remind humanity that the Church only exists to make Christ known and that this should be clearly visible for all to see by not only by what we do but how we do it. In the end what we find at Our Lady of the Wayside is a remarkable building with an atmosphere of beauty, harmony and peace, which even after all these years, continues to speak to the human spirit of the things of God.

A Personal Reflection to Finish

I first walked in through the doors of Our Lady of the Wayside Church in 1993 and I was ordained to the permanent diaconate there on 23rd May 2004 by Bishop Philip Pargeter. There have been many times since when I have reflected, personally, on the importance and meaning of the Church building for me. Now as I come to the end of what has been a three-book project I just want to make a couple of final points. The first concerns the Narthex or the porch of the Church. This for me is where everything begins both physically and spiritually. We physically enter the Church from the Stratford Road as we step through the impressive glass doors and our spiritual journey begins when we are baptised at the font in the baptistery. Here we become members of the Church, the body of Christ on earth and receive his most precious gift of new life. Pausing at the **'The Crucified Christ,'** we call to mind the words of our Lord as he journeys with us through life, **'Anyone who would be a follower of mine must take up his cross and follow me.'** (Matthew 16:24) How true those words are as each of us calls to mind the struggles we all have in just living. Yet this is the pattern for all of us that the cross always comes before the resurrection. Through the glass doors in front of us, however, we can see the resurrected Lord, above the altar, bursting out of the tomb still bearing the wounds of his cruel death. As we enter the main body of the Church our eyes cannot help but focus on the **'Risen Christ,'** the God who knows our pain and suffering because he has shared directly in them, comes in search of us, to find us because he loves us. Beneath this victorious figure is the impressive altar where the mass is celebrated so that God can share his life with us, where once again the brokenness of the **Crucified God** will heal the world and in so doing restore his people to the fullness of life. Little wonder, therefore, that the only response to this is to fall to our knees.

So to end, I share three experiences of my own with you. The first comes from my encounter with Mary and her Son Jesus, carved out of a single block of teak wood in the Lady Chapel. Here we find the figure of an ordinary woman and her child emerging out of the harsh reality of life. To say, **'yes'** to God could not have been easy for such a young girl and the price she had to pay would be a high one that would cost her much but despite this she was still able to say, **'Be it unto me according to your word.'** (Luke 1:38) It was this encounter with Our Lord through the bravery, love and absolute devotion of his Mother that inspired me to write my first book, **'Born for Us – A Journey into the Real Meaning of Christmas.'** In particular I refer to chapter thirteen, **'Our Lady of the Wayside – who are you?'** which emerged out of a deep period of prayer and reflection before this striking, intimate and extremely moving figure of Mary and her Son. I would draw your attention, in particular, to the way in which the child Jesus clings, lovingly, to the neck of his Mother and the way she, in turn, holds her close to him. It is as if the two can never be separated and it occurred to me that this is how God regards our relationship with him.

For my second experience I would take you back into the Narthex to stand in front of the **'Crucified Christ'** so clearly falling out of the wall in absolute agony. Once again, this image spoke so profoundly and powerfully to me in so far as it said that there was literally nothing that God was not prepared to go through for us. Yet that was not all, there was something else, which punctured my heart and compelled me to write my second book, **'Only in the Crucified God – Questions and Answers on Faith, Hope and Love,'** and it is this, that Christ shares everything we experience, every pain, every tear, every stumble, every fall – there is nothing that God, through his Son, does not share in directly with us. This is nothing less than the **Crucified God**, the God who comes in search of us, the God who will not stop until he finds each and every single one of us, the God who is willing to pay any price and do literally anything, for one reason and one reason only because he loves us more than we could ever know!

Now we come to my final experience, which is an encounter with the Risen Lord. Time really needs to be spent in the presence of God simply allowing him to love us. The figure of the '**Risen Christ**,' still bearing those terrible wounds, served to remind me of something but equally became the source of what I can only describe as a revelation. The wounds call to mind, that what happened to Jesus was real, he suffered and he died. However, through his resurrection those same wounds are transformed, they do not disappear but are changed by God's love, which is more powerful than hate and stronger than death. The resurrection of Christ is about life not death and it is life, God's life that He offers to us, now. Putting it another way through the resurrection of his Son from the dead God invites us to participate in his resurrected life in the here and now. It was this realisation that inspired me to write this book, the final one in the series, '**Sharing in the Life of God – A Journey into the Real Meaning of Easter.**'

In our busy and hectic lives it can be tempting and so easy not to take the time to stop and just be present in the moment. The parish Church of Our Lady of the Wayside provides those who visit it with the opportunity to step out of the demands of everyday life and to just experience the love of God. For me, the truth is that God is closer to us than we could ever imagine and loves us more than we could ever know. This same God is always present, never absent, just waiting for us to feel and experience his all-embracing love. Why not therefore pay us a visit and spend some time in the presence of the God of absolute and unconditional love, after all who knows what might happen?

This now brings my journey to an end, at least for now, but who knows what God might hold in store for the future? In conclusion though what I would say is this. Please come and visit us at Our Lady of the Wayside where everyone is more than welcome, you never know, it might just change your life!

May Our Lady of the Wayside, pray for us all now and always.

Deacon Sean

January 2021

ABOUT THE AUTHOR

Sean Loone is a Roman Catholic Deacon working in the Archdiocese of Birmingham. He has spent much of his career teaching in a variety of schools and colleges combining this with lecturing part-time at Saint Mary's College Oscott, the seminary for the Archdiocese. Currently he acts as chaplain and Religious Education advisor to a number of academic establishments including Our Lady of the Wayside, his home parish, where he is also the Catholic Life governor. His academic interests, on which he has published many articles, include Biblical studies and Christology. His most recent publication was a book called, **'Only in the Crucified God – Questions and Answers on Faith, Hope and Love.'** He also has extensive pastoral and sacramental experience combining this with a ministry dedicated to proclaiming God's word through both preaching and teaching the scriptures. He is married with three sons and is currently working on a new project, which aims, this time, to explore what it means to be a servant of the word.

BY THE SAME AUTHOR

Having completed my first book, **'Born For Us – A Journey into the Real Meaning of Christmas,'** I casually shared with my family my desire to write a second, **'Only in the Crucified God – Questions and Answers on Faith, Hope and Love.'** My son James replied by saying, 'Sounds like a trilogy to me.' Little did he or indeed I know then that this is exactly what would happen but it was at that precise moment in time that the seed was sown. This book is the final part of what James referred to as 'the trilogy.' The first book focused attention on the birth of Jesus, the second on his death and the impact it has on our lives, whilst the third would bring the so called trilogy to a conclusion by exploring the resurrection and the real meaning of Easter. In this way the three most important aspects of the Christian faith and the life of Jesus are explored and their meaning, as far as that is possible, explained. I never intended to write three books, in fact I never intended to write one but God moves, as they say in mysterious ways and here now is the culmination of a life of prayer, study and reflection. I commend the books to you, the reader, in the hope that they may help you deepen your knowledge and understanding of the God who loves you more than you could ever know.

The Birth of Jesus

'Born For Us – A Journey into the Real Meaning of Christmas'

Published by ALIVE Publishing

The Death of Jesus

'Only In the Crucified God – Questions and Answers on Faith, Hope and Love'

Published by Amazon

The Resurrection of Jesus

'Sharing In the Life of God – A Journey into the Real Meaning of Easter'

Published by Amazon

CREDITS

Front Cover artwork – Sophie Hobbs

Technical Advisor – Thomas Loone

In Loving Memory of

Father Paddy O'Mahony

Parish Priest

Our Lady of the Wayside

1962-1991

'Need not Creed'

Fr. Paddy O'Mahony

'For I was hungry and you gave me food, I was thirsty and you gave me drink, I was a stranger and you made me welcome, lacking clothes and you clothed me, sick and you visited me, in prison and you came to see me'

(Matthew 25: 35-37)

Jesus Christ

Is this the End?

'As for Mary, she treasured all these things and pondered them in her heart.' (Luke 2:19)

All the way through the pages of this book I have emphasised the importance of seeing the scriptures as a dialogue or putting it another way as a conversation between God and ourselves. Here I call to mind something I wrote previously, that through his word God speaks, we listen and then we are invited to respond. What, I wonder, might God be inviting us to do now? Perhaps, we will never know this side of heaven but this does not mean we ever stop trying. Yet the first thing we really need to learn to do is simply listen and recognise just how hard that can be. The key, of course, to unlocking the scriptures is Christ and it is to him we must turn if we are ever going to make any kind of progress. However, it is also vitally important that we see the word of God not as something from the past but as something alive and dynamic in the present speaking directly to us through our own experiences in the here and now. So for inspiration and a role model I turn finally to Mary, mother of Jesus. In his Gospel Luke describes how Mary simply **'treasured God's word in the depths of her heart,'** allowing them to penetrate deep into her very soul. I can think of no better way of describing of what our attitude to the scriptures should be. Ultimately, if like Mary we treasure God's word in the depths of our own hearts we might just find that we are led by Christ to something we could never have imagined before our journey began – transformed existence.

Deacon Sean January 2021